THE DAY THAT
Changed
America

Bob Fraley

Copyright 2008
Robert R. Fraley
All rights reserved
ISBN 978-09612999-6-5

Published by
Christian Life Outreach
P.O. Box 31129
Phonix, Arizona 85046-1129
www.christianlifeoutreach.org
www.campaignsaveamerica.com
www.theremarkablerevelation.com

Printed in the Republic of South Korea

ACKNOWLEDGEMENT

I wish to acknowledge my wife Barbara, our three children, the six children we took into our home to raise, their spouses, our grandchildren and their spouses, and our great grandchildren for their support. Presently the number in our family is 56 and everyone, except for the few who are still too young, has made a commitment to serve the Lord and has remained faithful. We continue to stay close as a family, visiting frequently and sharing many of our activities.

My friend Bob Fraley doesn't approach Scripture the way a trained Bible scholar normally would. And I have come to believe that therein lies his greatest strength. He thinks out of the box!

He has an incredible mind that has brought him remarkable success in the business world. I think of myself as relatively intelligent, but when he talks about his aerospace alloy aluminum-extrusion business, it's not long before I'm struggling to understand. That's even when he's trying to make things simple for me.

Bob can focus on a given topic with great tenacity. Then again, his mind sometimes makes strange leaps that land him in territories connected to what's being talked about, but I'm not always sure how. Over time I have learned to allow for these peculiar jumps because they can be quite productive. At any rate, I believe it is this maverick mental quality that has enabled him as a layman to come up with some breakthrough thinking regarding Bible prophecy.

Allow me to restate that. I don't believe Bob has ever said, "I have decided to systematically study the Book of Revelation, including what the early church fathers had to say about it, plus the contemporary theologians." If my memory serves me correctly, one of the first things I recall hearing him say to me was, "For over thirty-five years I've been interested in the beast Satan gives his authority to in Revelation 13."

The truth is, zeroing in on that specific chapter isn't a bad game plan. It's helpfully restrictive when looking at a confusing text like Revelation, while at the same time relating to one of the most important of the numerous visions given John by our Lord. Actually, it's the same approach he takes in this short book, and one of the reasons you will find it very readable.

The other is that his fresh thinking quickly captures your imagination. Whether or not you agree with all he writes, you are forced to carefully consider his convictions. They not only make good sense, their implications require that you rethink how you live. In a day when the religious beliefs of Americans are not all that high on the list of what motivates them, what Bob has to say is like a spiritual hand that grabs your backbone through your stomach and shakes you around a bit.

I see his words as a great gift for which all of us should be thankful. I admit that my great respect for the man colors my thinking. But I believe that even if you have never met him, through his words you will sense that he walks with the Lord and has certainly been given a message from Him for the greater Christian public.

Dr. David R. Mains
Mainstay Ministries

DR. DAVID MAINS: For over three decades, ministers have looked to Dr. David R. Mains as their friend. Many consider him to be a master teacher of effective preaching. Over the years, he has repeatedly proven his ability to help men and women become life-changing speakers. His background includes a decade of senior pasturing in Chicago at Circle Church, twenty years as Director of the "Chapel of the Air" radio ministry, winning the 1995 National Religious Broadcasters Programmer of the Year award, conceptualizing and writing "50 Day Spiritual Adventures" used by over 50,000 churches and more than 5 million people, as well as authoring over 20 books, including Gold Medallion Award winners.

CONTENTS

1

THE EVENT THAT CHANGED AMERICA FOREVER

For young children, December is a magical month. I was only seven and had already begun counting how much longer it was until Christmas. When I went to bed on Saturday evening, there were only 19 days to go. What I wanted to find under the tree more than anything else was a new pair of shoes.

That may sound strange, but the Great Depression had made an indelible impression on my parents' generation. Historians credit it with lasting almost the entire decade of the 1930s. The truth is, it was not only unprecedented in its length, but also in the wide poverty mentality it inflicted upon the general public.

At its worst, a staggering 25% of the country's labor force was without work. In our nation's cities thousands of people built makeshift shelters in empty lots, and garbage dumps were regularly scavenged by the hungry in search of food.

The year was 1941. Our president was Franklin Delano Roosevelt. An extremely popular and decisive chief executive, this was his third term in office. The world was at war, but America had stayed out of it. After World War I, we had strong misgivings about again sending our soldiers to fight in Europe's battles.

Not long after the fall of France to the Nazis in 1940, however, Congress began to take action, at least regarding our own national defense. The president was talking about a production goal of 50,000 fighter planes a year. To most people this sounded like a staggering number. The U.S. also started manufacturing war supplies for purchase by countries now threatened by the Axis powers of Germany and Italy.

Even an impartial observer would have said the outlook in Europe was bleak. Hitler controlled just about all of the western countries. England remained unconquered but was considered vulnerable. And now the Führer's armies had advanced hundreds of miles on the eastern front into Russia, which also appeared to be on the brink of collapse.

Equally unsettling news was coming out of the Far East. Japan, already at war with China, joined the Axis in 1940 and was aggressively moving on many fronts. Tokyo had recently announced it was establishing a joint protectorate over Indochina with Vichy France—the Nazi puppet state. Rumors were that General Hideki Tojo, the new prime minister, next wanted to take the Philippines and eventually even attack India. Names of U.S. missionaries taken captive in newly conquered Asian countries were also a grave concern to sponsoring church groups.

So all in all, it was a nervous time. Nevertheless, the truth was that most Americans saw these battles as faraway, and they wanted to keep things that way. Many in our country still remained quite isolationist in their thinking. We were a humble, peace-loving, Christian nation that deplored war and was extremely reluctant to get involved once more in its killing fields.

It was enough to get used to the fact that FDR had signed the Selective Training and Service Act—the first time there had been a military draft when the country was not engaged in actual warfare.

All of this, of course, went totally by me. I'm sure my parents talked about these issues, but I was too young to pay attention to their conversations. The morning of December 7, 1941, however, changed my world and that of all Americans in a most profound way. On that day, millions across the States huddled around their radios to hear the news. Confusion, disbelief and shock spread across the land. America had been attacked for the first time in more than a century. The Japanese had bombed Pearl Harbor. An unthinkable event had taken place … a day that would change America, forever.

PRELUDE TO THE ATTACK

In the spring of 1940, a large segment of the U.S. Pacific Fleet was stationed at Pearl Harbor. It was the world's greatest aggregation of warships—a million tons of fighting steel. But the U.S. influence in the Pacific irritated the Japanese. While European nations fought each other in the '30s, this island empire saw a golden opportunity to expand into Southeast Asia. But Japan feared our significant naval presence in the Pacific threatened their ambitious plans.

So in December 1940, Fleet Admiral Isoroku Yamamoto, Commander in Chief of Japan's Combined Fleet, convinced the Japanese Imperial Council to consider using their aircraft carriers to launch a surprise attack against the Pacific Fleet at Pearl Harbor. He reasoned that for Japan to achieve supremacy on the high seas, it had to neutralize America's military capacity.

Yamamoto's plan was to catch us sleeping—literally. He knew that just as a weaker judo expert can throw a stronger opponent by catching him off balance, Japan needed to seize the initiative. By striking a fatal blow in one daring attack, Yamamoto hoped to gain the military edge in the Pacific for a year. He and his advisors concluded that if Japan gained such an advantage for 12 months, they could win the war in the Pacific against the United States.

Yamamoto's idea had merit! And the majority of people in America were caught completely off-guard. A statement made on February 19, 1941 by Pennsylvania Congressman Charles I. Faddis sums up the United States' perspective. He declared:

> *The Japanese are not going to risk a fight with a first-class nation. They are unprepared to do so,*

and no one knows that better than they do. They will not dare to get into a position where they must face the American Navy in open battle. Their Navy is not strong enough and their homeland is too vulnerable.

It took a year of intense preparations for the Japanese to get ready. This planning had to be done in the strictest secrecy. If the strike did not catch the United States napping, the plan would fail.

The Japanese strategic military planners had several problems to solve before they could launch the mission. They had to design and build special torpedoes capable of operating in the shallow waters of Pearl Harbor; produce new armor-piercing shells that planes could deliver from low altitudes; select and train pilots on how to fly in low and attack such an area; and organize a naval task force and teach the personnel how to refuel the ships in the rough seas of the northern Pacific Ocean—the route selected to avoid detection and assure complete surprise. This Pearl Harbor plan was the most highly classified, closely guarded and best-kept secret of World War II, prior to the Manhattan Project (our development and dropping of the atomic bomb).

At 6 o'clock on the morning of November 26, 1941, the Japanese strike force weighed anchor. Eleven days later, just before dawn on December 7, they reached the launching point for their raid: 230 miles due north of the island of Oahu, Hawaii. Their task force of 33 warships, including six aircraft carriers, had successfully sailed a northern route through rough waters and dense fog to avoid detection by American ships and surveillance aircraft.

DECEMBER 7, 1941

The attack that Sunday morning came with startling swiftness. On every Japanese carrier, the scene was the same. The engines sputtered to life; up fluttered the signal flag and down again, as one by one the aircraft roared down the flight decks, drowning out the cheers and yells from the crews. Plane after plane rose in the sky, flashing in the early morning sun that peeked over the horizon. This airborne armada consisted of 353 planes. At the time it was the largest concentration of airpower in the history of warfare. On the peaceful target island, American sailors were totally unaware of the tremendous fighting force that would soon send many of them to a watery grave.

Perfect timing was essential. Our enemy knew full well that if anything went wrong, the attack could fail. But they were dead on course. Their mission: destruction of the Pacific Fleet stationed at Pearl Harbor and all of the nearby U.S. Air Force installations.

It was 7:40 a.m. when the first Japanese pilots sighted Oahu's coastline. Mitsuo Fuchida, the commander who led the first formation of planes (he became a Christian after the war), later wrote: "The harbor was still asleep in the morning mist." The element of surprise remained with the Japanese.

As the first wave of planes approached Pearl Harbor, they deployed into three groups. They first struck the air bases so our fighter planes could not get off the ground to counterattack the bombing of Pearl Harbor. They hit Hickam Air Force Base, Wheeler Field, Bellows Field, Kaneohe Naval Base and the Naval Air Station at Ford Island.

The Japanese pilots flew in at treetop level, bringing with them massive destruction. Hangars were burned, barracks were razed, and hundreds of men were killed that fateful morning. A total of 341 U.S. planes were destroyed while still on the ground. Since the air bases were so close together, the attacks all came at the same time. Everything happened at once.

But the assault on the airfields was only the start of the awful drama. In the harbor were 96 warships of the United States Pacific Fleet. Included were 8 cruisers, 29 destroyers, 5 submarines, assorted minecraft and 8 U.S. battleships: the *West Virginia*, *Arizona*, *Oklahoma*, *Nevada*, *Tennessee*, *Pennsylvania*, *California* and *Maryland*.

At approximately 8:10 a.m. the battleship *USS Arizona* exploded, having been hit by a 1760-pound armor-piercing bomb that slammed through her deck and ignited the main fuel tank. The force of the explosion was so great it raised the bow of the ship completely out of the water and split her right behind the number-one gun turret. She sank in less than nine minutes. Of her crew of 1543 men, 1177 lost their lives.

USS Arizona[1]

The *USS Oklahoma*, struck by several torpedoes, rolled completely over, trapping some 400 men inside. The *California* and *West Virginia* sank at their moorings, while the *Utah*, which had been converted to a training ship, capsized with more than 50 of her crew. The *Maryland*, *Pennsylvania* and *Tennessee* all suffered significant damage. The *Nevada* attempted to run out to sea but took several hits and had to be beached to avoid sinking and blocking the harbor entrance.

As the Japanese dive-bombers rocked the harbor, the mammoth gray ships along Battleship Row, writhing from the explosions of bombs and torpedoes, burned at their moorings, sending billows of black smoke into the morning sky. The invaders dealt crippling blows to ship after ship. Most of the damage was done in the first 15 minutes.

The attack on Pearl Harbor ended at about 9:45 a.m. In less than two hours the Japanese had immobilized most of our air strength and nearly eliminated their chief objective, the U.S. Pacific Fleet. A once-mighty military fortress had been pulverized. As the drone of enemy formations disappeared over the horizon, heading back to their carriers, they left behind a scene of horrible chaos—crackling flames, hissing steam and dying men. Half-submerged ships were strewn about the harbor, tilting at crazy angles. Wreckage floated across the oily surface of the water as human bodies began to wash ashore.

As the smoke began to clear, U.S. forces began to assess the damage. Twenty-two ships, including eight battleships, were sunk or heavily damaged, and more than 340 American aircraft had been destroyed. Japanese losses totaled 29 aircraft destroyed and 74 damaged. America had suffered one of the greatest defeats any nation ever endured at the beginning of a war. On the other hand, in a couple of hours the Japanese had seemingly secured mastery of the Far East.

It is difficult to overstate the importance of naval power prior to this age of aviation and nuclear weapons. Ships represented the ultimate in technological achievement. Battleships were the mightiest weapons of war, and luxury liners represented the epitome of Western culture. When a great ship sank—the *Lusitania*, the *Bismarck*, or the *Titanic*—people listened to the details in amazement. Such occasions inspired legends, ballads and movies. Sinking ships were cataclysmic events akin to natural disasters like earthquakes and hurricanes. In a matter of hours, the United States at Pearl Harbor had an unthinkable 22 ships either sunk or damaged.

THE AFTERMATH

Historians refer to this attack as one of the great turning points in world history. At the time, Hitler himself viewed this defeat as a mortal wound to our military strength, and on December 11 declared war on the United States. General Tojo was convinced that the war, for all practical purposes, was over. But instead, the attack on Pearl Harbor jarred the United States into astonishing activity. Here was a catalytic moment that eventually would spell defeat for the Axis.

In his memoirs, Winston Churchill wrote later that to now have the United States on England's side was to him the greatest of joys.

> *Hitler's fate was sealed. Mussolini's fate was sealed. As for the Japanese, they would be ground to powder. ... United we could subdue everybody else in the world. Many disasters, immeasurable cost and tribulation lay ahead, but there was no more doubt about the end.*

The next day, President Roosevelt asked Congress to declare war on Japan. His request carried almost unanimously. His famous words to the American public: "Yesterday, December 7, 1941—a date which will live in infamy—the United States of America was suddenly and deliberately attacked by naval and air forces of the Empire of Japan."

Earlier, on the afternoon of the attack, First Lady Eleanor Roosevelt had talked to the nation by radio:

> *For months now, the knowledge that something of this kind might happen has been hanging over our heads. ... We now know what we have to face, and we know we are ready to face it. Whatever is ahead of us, I am sure we can accomplish it; we are the free and unconquerable people of the United States of America.*

Almost immediately, men in every state formed long lines at draft boards, clamoring to join in the service of their country. As U.S. soldiers marched off to war, victory gardens sprang up, recycling bins appeared, and gas-rationing cards were introduced. Factories that produced autos were converted into making jeeps, tanks and airplanes. The attack that was supposed to be fatal actually energized the fighting spirit of Americans as little else could have done. The United States jumped to its feet to become a fearsome warrior. During the next three and a half years, we forged a war machine that helped conquer enemy forces on two different fronts, in Europe and Asia. America was transformed from a provincial, regional power to a technological, military and political titan stretching across both hemispheres, forever changing the American way of life.

To understand what happened at Pearl Harbor, and what led up to it, the book *At Dawn We Slept* by

Gordon W. Prange is considered by many to be the final word. His work has been praised as "definitive," "a masterpiece," "authoritative," "unparalleled" and "impossible to forget."

Prange was uniquely qualified for writing this book. He was educated at the University of Iowa and the University of Berlin. Later, he taught history at the University of Maryland. From October 1946 to June 1951, Prange was chief of General Douglas MacArthur's G-2 Historical Section located at General HQ, Far East Command, Tokyo.

From his training and firsthand knowledge, Prange knew more about the attack on Pearl Harbor than any other person. He also interviewed virtually every surviving Japanese officer who took part in the Pearl Harbor operation, as well as all pertinent sources on the U.S. side. His 873-page history of the attack is based on 37 years of research. His work is acclaimed worldwide and is an invaluable reference. It was used as a major source in making the movie *Tora! Tora! Tora!*

He writes:

> *The Japanese gave each American a personal stake in the titanic struggle for the minds and bodies of mankind [that] raged in Europe and Asia. After December 7, 1941, Americans no longer could look upon the war from a distance as an impersonal, ideological conflict. The sense of outrage triggered a feeling of direct involvement [that] resulted in an explosion of national energy. The Japanese gave the average American a cause he could understand and believe to be worth fighting for. Thus, in a very*

special way Pearl Harbor became the turning point of the world struggle.

The attack was so sudden, so spectacular and so devastating; Congress convened a joint committee to investigate. The committee's findings filled 40 volumes. <u>This single attack set into motion forces that changed forever the way Americans work, play, build families and conduct their lives. Our involvement in the war transformed our land from a provincial, isolationist country to a superpower—a technological hothouse of incredible economic, political and military power.</u>

A Tragedy Remembered

Our 41st President George Bush journeyed to Hawaii on December 7, 1991, to revisit Pearl Harbor on the 50th anniversary of the attack. The years have slipped by quickly, and new generations of Americans have all but forgotten the tragedy of Pearl Harbor. However, for any who visit that site, it remains a grim reminder of a defeat that shoved our country into the fierce vortex of sacrifice, suffering and war. What happened that day will live forever through the *Arizona* Memorial, dedicated on Memorial Day, 1962.

Today, the *USS Arizona* rests peacefully in an upright position under 38 feet of water at the bottom of Pearl Harbor. Visitors stand atop the wreckage to look down at the remains of the sunken ship. Oil still rises from her rusting hull, and the 1100 men still entombed there provide a silent but eloquent witness to the horror of defeat.

Arizona Memorial Spans Sunken USS Arizona[1]

The memorial was designed with a sag in the middle. Solid white walls and a roof compose two ends of the rectangular building, exposing a thin archway of bare, white ribs. The depressed center was purposely designed to express the initial wound to a great nation, and the sturdy ends to express its earlier strength and eventual recovery and victory.

There can be little doubt but that this was a defining event that forever changed who we are as a people. It's not like an earlier version of 9/11/01. It's far and beyond the scope of that day, as awful as it was. It was Pearl Harbor that also put the United States on a path that would lead almost inevitably to us becoming the world's great superpower! Allow me to unpack that claim in Chapter 2.

Arizona Memorial[1]

2

SEVEN DECADES LATER

On December 7, 2011, it will be seven decades since that "date which will live in infamy." The charismatic president who spoke those words died in April of 1945. Since then, America has had 11 new chief executives: Truman, Eisenhower, Kennedy, Johnson, Nixon, Ford, Carter, Reagan, Bush Sr., Clinton, and G. W. Bush.

After Pearl Harbor, Admiral Isoroku Yamamoto oversaw the Japanese fleet in the critical Battle of Midway. After further engagements at Guadalcanal, he planned to tour some of his country's forward bases. Unaware that we had cracked the Japanese code and knew his agenda, he was shot down by American fighter planes in April of 1943. He died in the crash.

General Tojo, who along with Hitler and Mussolini personified the Axis powers to most people around the world, was forced out of power when the U.S. took Saipan, which put us within bombing range of Japan. After the war, when he learned he would be put on trial, Tojo tried unsuccessfully to take his life. A number of high-ranking Japanese military officers were charged with atrocities, crimes against peace and crimes against humanity. Their trial lasted almost three years. Tojo was among seven who were sentenced to death by hanging.

At the end of the war, Russia took over much of Eastern Europe. Living up to the name he had assumed, Stalin ("Man of Steel") was ambitious in his efforts to enhance the spread of communism. A "Cold War" quickly developed between the East and West, and it continued even after his death in 1953.

Churchill fell from political power before the war with Japan was over, only to be asked to once again assume the role of Prime Minister in 1951. He would live a long and productive life, and die an international hero in 1965.

If to some these recollections seem far removed from today's headlines, that's understandable. Time passes quickly, and it seems even important leaders are here today and gone tomorrow. It would also be a daunting task to put together a definitive list of important changes in our world over the past 70 years. The United States is certainly a vastly different nation than it was in 1941 on that day that changed America. Allow me to paint that picture for you with a broad brush.

PROSPEROUS

The United States was just recovering from the Great Depression in 1941 when she had to suddenly shift to a war mentality. With the needed production of all kinds of military hardware, unemployment was no longer a problem. Labor lived up to its non-strike pledges because something more important than wages and working conditions was at stake. Farmers enjoyed the best markets in decades, and numbers of them got out of debt.

Following victory, the first matter facing the U.S. was to demobilize the armed forces and revert industry from wartime production back to normal peacetime operations. In our favor was a huge demand for American products abroad. The nations of Europe and Asia, powerful before the war, were ravaged by its devastation. Years of fighting had demolished their cities, pulverized their industry and robbed them of a generation of their best and brightest young people.

None of the fighting had occurred on American soil though, so we emerged as the only power with its industrial base intact. As a result, our factories were uniquely able to furnish wartime allies with many of the products and services their people so badly needed. During the next 30 years, U.S. exports fueled a fantastic economic boom.

By way of contrast, World War II left the countries of Europe and the Pacific Rim in shambles. Many people lost not only their homes but also their means of livelihood. The fighting destroyed factories, power plants, businesses, roads, bridges, rail lines and much more. Germany, England, France, Japan, Russia and numerous other nations lost much of their industrial capacity. The infrastructure needed for economic productivity had also been wiped out by war.

Consequently, the economic strength of these nations suffered a severe setback. For example, England's financial and political power never returned to the previous status quo. It went from being an industrial giant with global interests to a more internally focused nation with a moderate role to play in international affairs. So while other former powers crawled out from under the rubble of the war, the United States was on its way to economic supremacy.

All this allowed the average American worker to have a steady job and a good income. Few countries in the industrialized world could boast higher pay, more extensive fringe benefits or better working conditions.

American companies captured first place in the production of automobiles, machine tools, electronic equipment, and many other vital industries. Our output of quality agricultural goods was unsurpassed. This also created an impressive trade surplus. Year after year, following the war, Americans sold far more overseas than they bought, and billions of excess dollars from abroad poured into our economy.

As a result, the average American family claimed possessions that were unprecedented in the history of mankind. The U.S. made up 7% of the world's population, yet we held half of the world's wealth and were responsible for an entire third of the world's total yearly consumption of resources. From a material standpoint,

Americans lived better than virtually all other people on the globe. This was certainly not our position back in 1941.

POWERFUL

Toward the close of the war, the United States launched a surprise attack of its own against Japan. The Manhattan Project consisted of a team of top scientists working on a superweapon in an isolated part of the Southwestern U.S. It was tested successfully for the first time near Alamogordo, New Mexico on July 16, 1945. The massive explosion stunned even its creators.

President Truman, informed of the results, was advised that using the atomic bomb against Japan could potentially save a half-million American troops. That's the number of casualties the military experts projected, were we to invade the Japanese mainland.

The first bomb, codenamed *Little Boy,* was dropped on the port city of Hiroshima on August 6, 1945. The destruction was unimaginable. More than 70,000 were killed by the initial blast, and at least that many later died from radiation poisoning. Practically everything within a one-mile radius of the center of the explosion just spontaneously combusted. Large buildings disappeared. Human beings were vaporized. Reports of what happened shocked the world.

Soon after, a second, slightly different-style bomb, called *Fat Man,* was dropped on Nagasaki, a shipbuilding center. Almost half the city was instantaneously annihilated. An estimated 40,000 were killed, with almost double that number dead within a year from radiation sickness.

This incredible new weapon brought a quick end to a long war. American, British and Russian troops shared handshakes and hugs, but it wasn't long before the free world and countries of the Soviet Bloc began to view each other as enemies.

Though Russia was indebted to us for massive aid during the war, Stalin turned on his friends and became the next threat to world peace. With the help of top Nazi scientists who were prisoners of war, the Soviets detonated an atomic bomb of their own in September of 1949.

Not to be outdone, on November 1, 1952 the U.S. exploded the first hydrogen bomb at Eniwetok Atoll in the Pacific Ocean. It was brighter than ten suns; the fireball was three miles wide and a thousand feet high. Its force was equal to 20 million tons of TNT. It was estimated this bomb could devastate an area of 300 square miles by its blast, and 1200 square miles by the resultant fire. In short, we had invented something so powerful it could obliterate any major city in the world!

Ten months later, the Russians detonated a hydrogen bomb of their own. Then in the spring of 1954, the U.S. exploded a bomb one hundred times more destructive than any previous manmade explosion.

America now had weapons like no other military force in history. Whereas our newfound strength made us secure, it terrified other nations. This only served to elevate the arms race that finally ended with the dissolution of the Soviet Union in 1991.

In the meantime, at least seven other nations have come, in one way or another, to possess nuclear warheads. None of them, however, has anywhere near the striking power and nuclear weaponry of the United States and her allies. The U.S. is arguably the sole remaining superpower, and it has every intention of keeping it that way. Such a claim would have been ludicrous in 1941.

Proud

All too often, with prosperity and power comes pride. Humility is not a common characteristic among the wealthy and mighty. Assuming they are the ones responsible for getting where they are, they start to swagger. This is true of nations as well as people.

Back in the days of the prophet Daniel, this was the path walked by pompous King Nebuchadnezzar. His city was splendid in every way. A massive ziggurat, the great Tower of Babel, stood in the temple area. Close by were the famous Hanging Gardens of Babylon, which the Greeks counted as one of the Seven Wonders of the World. It was about 600 years before the time of Christ, and Nebuchadnezzar's kingdom was recognized by everyone as the dominant superpower.

This king was both the ruler and the embodiment of the nation. In some ways he was like Saddam Hussein prior to the Gulf Wars. Incidentally, the ruins of ancient Babylon are close to present-day Baghdad in Iraq. Nebuchadnezzar's words were like a god's. To be his friend was a rare privilege; to be his enemy was your worst nightmare.

Scripture reveals how God attempted to warn this monarch about his pride. Daniel chapter 4 reads:

> *I, Nebuchadnezzar, was at home in my palace, contented and prosperous. I had a dream that made me afraid. As I was lying in my bed, the images and visions that passed through my mind terrified me. ... When the magicians, enchanters, astrologers and diviners came, I told them the dream, but they could not interpret it for me. Finally, Daniel came into my presence and I told him the dream. (He is called Belteshazzar, after the name of my god, and the spirit of the holy gods is in him.)*

> *I said, "Belteshazzar ... Here is my dream; interpret it for me. ... I looked, and there before me stood a tree in the middle of the land. ... The tree grew large and strong and its top touched the sky; it was visible to the ends of the earth. Its leaves were beautiful, its fruit abundant, and on it was food for all. Under it the beasts of the field found shelter, and the birds of the air lived in its branches; from it every creature was fed.*

> *"In the visions I saw while lying in my bed, I looked, and there before me was a messenger, a holy one, coming down from heaven. He called in a loud voice: 'Cut down the tree and trim off its branches; strip off its leaves and scatter its fruit. Let the animals flee from under it and the birds from its branches. But let*

the stump and its roots, bound with iron and bronze, remain in the ground, in the grass of the field.

"'Let him be drenched with the dew of heaven, and let him live with the animals among the plants of the earth. Let his mind be changed from that of a man and let him be given the mind of an animal, till seven times pass by for him.'"

If I had a similar dream, I believe I too would be upset.

Then Daniel ... was greatly perplexed for a time, and his thoughts terrified him. So the king said, "Belteshazzar, do not let the dream or its meaning alarm you."

Picture yourself having God reveal to you what this strange dream is about, and you then having to tell some cruel leader, like Saddam Hussein, a message he's not going to like all that much.

Belteshazzar (Daniel) *answered, "My lord, if only the dream applied to your enemies and its meaning to your adversaries! The tree you saw, which grew large and strong, with its top touching the sky, visible to the whole earth, with beautiful leaves and abundant fruit, providing food for all, giving shelter to the beasts of the field, and having nesting places in its branches for the birds of the air—you, O king, are that tree! You have become great and strong; your greatness has grown until it reaches the sky, and your dominion extends to distant parts of the earth.*

"You, O king, saw a messenger, a holy one, coming down from heaven and saying, 'Cut down the tree

and destroy it, but leave the stump, bound with iron and bronze. ... Let him live like the wild animals, until seven times pass by for him.'

"This is the interpretation, O king, and this is the decree the Most High has issued against my lord the king: You will be driven away from people and will live with the wild animals; you will eat grass like cattle, and be drenched with the dew of heaven. Seven times will pass by for you until you acknowledge that the Most High is sovereign over the kingdoms of men and gives them to anyone he wishes. The command to leave the stump of the tree with its roots means that your kingdom will be restored to you when you acknowledge that Heaven rules. Therefore, O king, be pleased to accept my advice: Renounce your sins by doing what is right, and your wickedness by being kind to the oppressed. It may be that then your prosperity will continue."

Nebuchadnezzar was glad to have the mystery solved, but he didn't take Daniel's advice to heart.

Twelve months later, as the king was walking on the roof of the royal palace of Babylon, he said, "Is not this the great Babylon I have built as the royal residence, by my mighty power and for the glory of my majesty?"

The words were still on his lips when a voice came from heaven, "This is what is decreed for you, King Nebuchadnezzar: Your royal authority has been taken from you. You will be driven away from people and will live with the wild animals; you will eat grass like cattle. Seven times will pass by for you until you acknowledge that the Most High is

> *sovereign over the kingdoms of men and gives them to anyone he wishes."*

> *Immediately what had been said about Nebuchadnezzar was fulfilled. He was driven away from people and ate grass like cattle. His body was drenched with the dew of heaven until his hair grew like the feathers of an eagle and his nails like the claws of a bird.*

This unusual passage actually has a rather remarkable ending.

> *My sanity was restored, my honor and splendor were returned to me for the glory of my kingdom. My advisers and nobles sought me out, and I was restored to my throne and became even greater than before. Now I, Nebuchadnezzar, praise and exalt and glorify the King of heaven, because everything he does is right and all his ways are just. And those who walk in pride he is able to humble.*

God is able to humble all those who walk in pride.

Nations are often a reflection of the collective thoughts of their people. I fear too many Americans today think, "Is not this the great country we have built by our strength and ingenuity? Remove those old notions about God from the history books our children study. To accept that He had a hand in making us great is a concept we should have set aside decades ago!"

PROFANE

Prosperous, powerful, proud and profane. That last word means to treat the sacred with an attitude of contempt. It's to dismiss religion as more or less irrelevant for moderns. It's a secular mindset that sets aside spiritual contributions as being for the most part meaningless. Profane can also go beyond ignoring the church to ridiculing and debasing it. Profanity, which has become increasingly acceptable in our culture, is an example of profane language.

It's almost as if there is an unstated national effort to distance ourselves from our religious past, and a new emphasis on tolerance demands that "Christian America" be thought of as a term that's outdated, embarrassing and even offensive.

In recent decades America has changed many of the standards that were held to since the founding of our country. These include the way we raise our families, run our schools, go about our business, set moral values and even go to war. All this has resulted in numerous societal adjustments that would once have been thought unthinkable.

Even our government has taken actions that never would have been considered by earlier generations. The most obvious example is the passing of laws that have allowed for the killing of millions of innocent babies through abortions on demand.

It's not surprising that a report covering a recent 30-year period shows crime had increased by 500%, illegitimate births by 400%. The teen suicide rate has tripled. Incest and child molestation have become a national concern; police estimate that just 25% of instances are reported. Enough teachers and students have been gunned down to make weapons checks commonplace in schools. The entertainment industry discovered it could display violence and sexually explicit scenes with minimal public resistance.

In fact, since World War II the most fundamental means of preserving order, which is commitment to the family, has taken hit after hit. The divorce rate has skyrocketed even among regular churchgoers. Greed and unethical conduct has tainted such professions as doctors, politicians, ministers, corporate executives, educators, lawyers, athletes and other pillars of society. Large areas of our great cities have turned into stalking grounds for gang violence, sexual perversions, crime and drug-dealing. We now have the largest prison population in the world, as our rate of incarceration is more than seven times higher than that of most other nations. Addiction to pornography has reached epidemic levels for both Christians and non-Christians. Our country, which had such a strong Christian foundation and where so much Christian teaching has taken place, has experienced an overwhelming increase in the spirit of lawlessness, permissiveness, rebellion and selfishness in this last generation. The percentage of young American adults who have biblically based values has dropped since WWII from 65% to 4%.

Is it too much to claim that the standards in our country have deteriorated more in this last generation than in all the previous ones since our forefathers founded America? In the history of mankind has there ever been a society where moral values have dropped so precipitously in such a short time period? And unfortunately, that trend shows no sign of turning around.

I also believe we are living in one of the toughest of times to be a committed follower of Jesus. The devil never had the opportunity to tempt people as easily as he does now. No longer does he have to lure us to some dimly lit part of town to show us his wares. He boldly comes right into our homes via the Internet, DVDs, TV, radio, CDs, magazines, books, you name it. His evil enticements are made conveniently available, and all too many Christians find his offerings attractive.

No, the U.S. is not the same country it was in 1941. Spiritually speaking, we have opened ourselves to attack. But the question is, what are we becoming?

In a way I would prefer not to give you my answer. The future is frightening. But silence is not an option the Lord has given me.

I'll explain more fully what I mean. But first let me tell you a little bit about myself.

3

LET'S GET ACQUAINTED

I am not a trained theologian. Nor do I think of myself as a preacher. Basically I am a Christian businessman who in the course of my spiritual formation developed an intense interest in Bible prophecy and America in these last days. In that regard I feel compelled to share some conclusions I believe God has impressed on my heart. I am not so opinionated, however, as to believe that I have the final word on this topic. All I am asking for is a fair hearing in the hopes that God will use this to motivate you to consider its implications on your life.

More specifically, my attention has been drawn to the identity of the beast in Revelation chapter 13. Verses 1-7a of that passage reads:

> *And I saw a beast coming out of the sea. He had ten horns and seven heads, with ten crowns on his horns, and on each head a blasphemous name. The beast I saw resembled a leopard, but had feet like those of a bear and a mouth like that of a lion. The dragon*

gave the beast his power and his throne and great authority. One of the heads of the beast seemed to have had a fatal wound, but the fatal wound had been healed. The whole world was astonished and followed the beast. Men worshiped the dragon because he had given authority to the beast, and they also worshiped the beast and asked, "Who is like the beast? Who can make war against him?"

The beast was given a mouth to utter proud words and blasphemies and to exercise his authority for forty-two months. He opened his mouth to blaspheme God, and to slander his name and his dwelling place and those who live in heaven. He was given power to make war against the saints and to conquer them.

Even as a layman, it's quite clear to me that this beast is a great world power that will someday make war against God's people. This passage has a similarity to the beasts the prophet Daniel saw in a vision, which is recorded in the seventh chapter of the Old Testament book that bears his name. Verses 4-6:

"The first was like a lion, and it had the wings of an eagle. I watched until its wings were torn off and it was lifted from the ground so that it stood on two feet like a man, and the heart of a man was given to it.

"And there before me was a second beast, which looked like a bear. It was raised up on one of its sides, and it had three ribs in its mouth between its teeth. It was told, 'Get up and eat your fill of flesh!'

> *"After that, I looked, and there before me was an-*
> *other beast, one that looked like a leopard. And on*
> *its back it had four wings like those of a bird. This*
> *beast had four heads, and it was given authority*
> *to rule."*

Since the beasts in that chapter are identified as kingdoms or world empires (verses 15-18) …

> *"I, Daniel, was troubled in spirit, and the visions that*
> *passed through my mind disturbed me. I approached*
> *one of those standing there and asked him the true*
> *meaning of all this.*
>
> *"So he told me and gave me the interpretation of*
> *these things: 'The four great beasts are four king-*
> *doms that will rise from the earth. But the saints of*
> *the Most High will receive the kingdom and will*
> *possess it forever—yes, for ever and ever.'"*

… it would appear consistent that this beast in Revelation is also a world kingdom. I will probably sound more like a businessman than a minister or Bible professor, but I see this beast as what most people today would call a superpower.

At present, the United States is the reigning superpower. Therefore, to me an obvious question to ask is, "Could our nation in some way be this beast?" Maybe it's the United States several years down the road. Possibly it's an alliance of the U.S. and her close allies.

Anyway, it seems wrong to just quickly assume this is not even a remote possibility, as we are the reigning superpower in these last days.

By asking this question I may have caught you off-guard. Just be aware that I am in no way anti-American. I love this country! I am patriotic and proud to be a citizen. America has been incredibly good to me in ever so many ways. It's just that this appears to be a natural starting point if modern world powers are being considered.

I have personally given this matter a great deal of thought, and I want to share my observations in careful detail. But before I do, I felt it would be good if you were better acquainted with me. I know I am usually less resistant to people's ideas when I have a bit of a handle on who they are, and where they are coming from. In telling my story, I want to underscore the kind and gracious manner in which God has consistently dealt with me. Everything I have been given or have accomplished I quickly acknowledge to be from His hand.

I was the last of 13 children. My father was a schoolteacher and a businessman, and he farmed in his later years. My mother was a contemporary example of the woman in Proverbs 31. Both my parents lived what they taught us about being followers of Christ. I made my first commitment to serve the Lord when I was nine, and I still remember being baptized in the muddy creek that cut through our farm.

After graduating from college I married Barbara, a Christian girl from my hometown. In those first few years of marriage, our spiritual commitment was not what it should have been. So we recommitted our lives to the Lord, making Him the center of all our activities, and I began to personally study the Bible and taught it at our church. Barbara was known as Mrs. Energy. Her gift of hospitality was soon put to use by the Lord. It would be difficult to recall the number of times we had from 25 to 150 people to our home for a sit-down dinner she served hot and fresh, with all the trimmings. This, along with her added gift to cheer the heart as good medicine (Proverbs 17:22), has been a blessing to many.

After my schooling I worked for Reynolds Aluminum Company in the sales division. I received their top industrial-sales award and had reached the level of District Sales Manager when, at 32, I was recruited by Benada Aluminum. I accepted the position of Vice President and General Manager. My business career was becoming well-established.

It was about five years after recommitting our lives to the Lord that on a lovely fall day in October of '69, one of the elders where we attended church and his wife were killed in a car accident. They had been the parents of six children! Over the next few weeks and through several miraculous interventions by the Lord, Barbara and I felt led to raise these children along with our own. Those six children, along with our own three, are now adults. They have each received a college education and have wonderful careers and families. Presently we have 56 in our family, including spouses, grandchildren and great-grandchildren. Everyone, except for the few who are still too young, has made a commitment to serve the Lord. We continue to stay close as a family, sharing many of our activities.

Here is a picture of me with Barbara and our nine children. It was taken on our 50th wedding anniversary. The three men in the back are our sons. The man at the left and the five women are the six we took as our own in 1969 after their parents were killed.

The Fraley's 50th wedding Anniversary with their children.

I had a major career change a few years after we enlarged our family. One of the girls was having a difficult time in high school. She was experiencing criticism both from students and certain teachers for her commitment to follow biblical standards. In seeking the Lord's counsel on how to help her, I was led to Psalm 1:1-3. It reads:

> *Blessed is the man who does not walk in the counsel of the wicked or stand in the way of sinners or sit in the seat of mockers. But his delight is in the law*

of the Lord, and on his law he meditates day and night. He is like a tree planted by streams of water, which yields its fruit in season and whose leaf does not wither. Whatever he does prospers.

Through these verses I was convicted that we were to take our children out of the public school system. At that time, the state where we lived did not allow private Christian schools. I resigned from my executive position, and Barbara and I began searching for where the Lord would have us move. Through a series of trips to different parts of the country we felt led to move to Phoenix, where we found a strong Christian high school and grade schools. By the end of January 1973, we had sold our house, packed our belongings in two U-Haul trucks and, like a small caravan, headed for Arizona. We made the move on faith. From our savings and the sale of our property we had the funds to make a down payment on a house, enroll the kids in Christian schools and live several months until I found employment.

I explored several job possibilities, but each time, the door closed. About seven months passed when I heard about an individual, Frank Labriola, who had received an SBA loan and was starting an aluminum-extrusion business near Phoenix. That was the same business I had resigned from as Vice President and General Manager. He needed someone with my experience but was concerned about the salary I might want. After discussing his business plans, I was convinced in my heart this was where the Lord wanted me. I told

Frank I didn't care what he paid me, even if it was $1000 per month. I would help him build a company and trust that he would make it up later.

Frank called in a few days and said he had reviewed his financial projections and could afford to pay me $1250 per month. Barbara and I were overwhelmed with how faithful the Lord was, in that here was an opportunity in my area of expertise. We reviewed our budget and discovered that the net I'd be receiving was almost to the penny what we'd need to meet our minimum living expenses. In the fall of 1973 I joined this new company called Pimalco. We made our first shipment of aluminum extrusions on November 30, 1973. About a year later Frank made me an officer and gifted me with an interest in the company.

By 1975 we had expanded our manufacturing facility to include the production of aerospace extrusions. This product is one of the materials used to build the structure of the body, wings and tail sections of airplanes. The requirements are the most stringent in the aluminum industry, and your process technology is continually audited and certified by every airplane manufacturer you supply. The metallurgical demands are so difficult that more than 75% of the companies that have attempted to produce this product have failed.

It became obvious to me the Lord's guidance was involved in the business decisions we made, as they consistently proved fruitful in manufacturing this difficult product. Over the next several years

Pimalco developed into one of the best aerospace-extrusion facilities in the world. Our success became well-known, and our company became an aggressive buyout target.

Due to some new high-tech aluminum alloys that had been developed, and the expense of obtaining them, in 1985 we decided to sell 51 percent of the company to Alcoa to obtain these patented alloys. Alcoa wanted an option to purchase the balance of the company in six years, and they did, stating we were the best operating subsidiary in their corporation. The company had expanded to sales of more than $100 million per year with an employment of more than 600. Frank and I stayed on in executive positions until June 30, 1995, when we retired.

Though I was only 60, Barbara and I thought my career in industry was over. But the Lord had other plans. Through a series of unexpected events, my retirement proved short-lived. In early '96, I got a call from an executive friend at Reynolds Aluminum. They'd been asked by Boeing to consider entering the aerospace-extrusion market. He wondered if I was interested in forming a joint venture with Reynolds to pursue this market. They had two extrusion presses that could be made available immediately along with the necessary auxiliary finishing equipment. The normal delivery time for a new extrusion press is about one year, and the cost per press is $1.5-$3 million depending on size.

Although I knew the president of Reynolds along with my friend, I was also familiar with how quickly management personnel in large corporations can change. So I declined the offer. Somewhat on a lark, I suggested to him that Reynolds sell me the presses and maybe I would enter the extrusions marketplace again on my own. He said he would present my suggestion to the board of directors. To my surprise he called back and said the board had approved selling me the equipment.

I sought the Lord for His guidance. I was going to wait on Him until I knew in my heart that I knew. One morning as I was walking and praying for His direction, I received what has only happened a few times in my life: a word from the Lord. He said, "I will bless the company."

This inspired me to put together a financial *pro forma* for the first five years of operation including cash flow projections for handling the cost of equipment, operations, marketing and office expenses, inventory and accounts receivable. I placed a startup value on the company and ventured out to see if I could raise about 20% of the large amount I would need plus my own funds to make a down payment on the equipment and provide the cash flow for the startup.

I was soon overwhelmed! Any new startup is high-risk, but I had more people wanting to invest than shares I wanted to sell.

I named the company ALEXCO, which stands for "aluminum-extrusion company." By the end of 1996 I had purchased the two presses from Reynolds and had most of the other factors in place. Word soon got around the industry that I was starting a new company to produce aerospace quality aluminum extrusions. Due to the difficulty in producing this high-tech product and being approved by the elite aerospace industry, there were only two other major manufacturers of this product in America, so experienced know-how was scarce.

Once again, the Lord began to move in a miraculous way. This time it was to develop a core of experienced management and supervisor personnel. I began to receive employment applications from some of the most experienced people in the industry. Everyone was informed that I would not pay more than they were presently making. That was not an issue with anyone. A management team was soon assembled, having some of the finest of experienced personnel in producing aerospace quality aluminum extrusions.

ALEXCO officially began on March 1, 1997 by taking over an existing Reynolds Aluminum plant in Torrance, California, where one of the extrusion presses I bought was located. Barbara and I rented a large apartment for our management team to live in during the week. Within five weeks we installed several additional items of finishing equipment for producing aerospace aluminum extrusions and converted the press to produce the same. With my relationships in the industry we were certified by Boeing and several other companies that build airplanes, and on April 21 we began production. Within three weeks the company had received enough business to operate at full production working 24 hours a day, six days a week.

By July, I broke ground on a new manufacturing and office facility in the Lone Butte Industrial Park, located in the Gila River Indian community, in Chandler, Arizona, a suburb of Phoenix. By January '98 we moved into our new facility. The Lord had truly blessed the company as He promised. At the end of 1998, 19 months after we had started production, ALEXCO was debt-free. Since then we have more than doubled our original plant and office size. All aspects of ALEXCO can be read about at our Web site, www. alexcoaz.com.

ALEXCO'S office and manufacturing facility.

ALEXCO has also been blessed by the Lord in other ways as well. For example, in 2004 we were selected by a large manufacturer of regional jet commercial aircraft to receive their 2003 Raw Material Supplier of the Year Award, competing with all of their material suppliers worldwide. Another blessing is that we were the first aerospace aluminum-extrusion company to be certified to the new, more stringent aerospace quality certification requirements. This made a huge statement to the entire aircraft-manufacturing industry.

Finally, I should mention that ALEXCO was selected as the U.S. Small Business Administration's 2005 Region IX Subcontractor of the Year. There are 10 regions in the country, and the competition for this prestigious award is keen. We were honored during the SBA Expo 2005 event, held at the Hilton Washington Hotel in our nation's capital.

To be considered for this award, each manufacturer is audited and graded in 10 categories. The first is Management (an assessment of the subcontractor's ability to organize and utilize its own resources to ensure accomplishment of business objectives). The other nine categories, without explanation, are: (2) Financial Stamina and Controls, (3) Labor Relations, (4) Customer Interface, (5) Technical Capabilities, (6) Resource Utilization, (7) Cost Performance, (8) Delivery Performance, (9) Quality Performance and (10) Overall Evaluation.

Each company nominated is graded on a 10-point scale in each category. A grade of 1 is considered satisfactory; 2 or 3 is good; 4, 5 or 6 is excellent; 7, 8, 9 or 10 is superior. ALEXCO got a 10 in every category!

President George W. Bush spoke at one of the Expo's luncheons, commenting that the small-business sector of the American economy is one of our country's great strengths. He also noted that small businesses are at the heart of America's growth, creating most new private-sector jobs. At ALEXCO we have around 200 employees.

Small Business Administration 2005 Region IX
Sub-Prime Contractor of the Year Award

A cover article about ALEXCO in the June, 1998 issue of *Light Metal Age*, the international magazine of the light-metal industry, included the following:

> *Fraley has a deep concern for the welfare of others, as is evidenced in his company's bylaws: A minimum of 10% of before-tax profit is annually given to help the poor and needy. The company is currently providing the funds for building part of a children's hospital in Kenya, East Africa, as well as feeding*

*and clothing inner-city families in this country, and
helping reduce poverty in Mexico.*

You can check out other projects we have funded
in Africa by visiting the Web site www.christian
lifeoutreach.org and clicking on "Help the World
Direct."

Apart from the grace of God I know my story
would be quite different. It is an understatement to
write that the Lord has been incredibly good to me and
that if there is any praise to be given, it must go first
and foremost to Him.

4

THE LAST GREAT SUPERPOWER

The beast that Satan gives his authority to in Revelation chapter 13 will no doubt be the greatest superpower in the history of the world. This makes a lot more sense than the devil forming an alliance with a second-or third-rate power.

America presently holds that position of supremacy. If she maintains this advantage, is it possible she also fits into the prophecy Jesus gave to John in the book of Revelation?

In the year 2007 I wrote a 281-page book, *Salt and Light*, that examines this question in detail. In this abbreviated version I intend to touch on some of the more significant points.

1. Satan is real and wars against everything related to God.

In Revelation 12:9 we are told: "The great dragon was hurled down—that ancient serpent called the devil, or Satan, who leads the whole world astray. He was hurled to the earth, and his angels with him." It's here on earth that he makes war against "those who obey God's commands and hold to the testimony of Jesus" (verse 17).

So the target of Satan's wrath is anyone who loves and serves the Lord. It has always been this way, and it always will be. This is a serious matter because the devil is a powerful and intelligent being. I'm not referring to a caricature of a bright-red scoundrel with horns, hoofs and pitchfork. Instead, I have in mind the one whom Jesus in all seriousness called a liar and a murderer.

Even now, the enemy derives special delight in undermining outstanding believers, churches and, would you believe, nations. The way he went after Job is typical and should serve as a warning to individuals. How many are the prominent churches he has ruined through his sinister ways? Old Testament Israel's apostasy as a nation also has his imprint all over it.

The spiritual roots of America run very deep. She is a country that has been blessed by the Lord in many ways. "America, America, God shed his grace on thee." With this in mind, we still need to be aware that the enemy would like nothing more than to change her allegiance from "one nation, under God" to "one nation, no longer under God."

Satan always viciously attacks anything that the Lord raises up. Can we suppose for one minute that he will leave unscathed a nation that has been so much a center of the faith that for generations it has been referred to as "Christian America"?

Key to this country's future are her many churches. When they are strong, the enemy is in trouble. When they are weak, his job is much easier. When congregations forget that their primary "struggle is not against flesh and blood, but ... against the spiritual forces of evil in the heavenly realms" (Ephesians 6:12), they are in a precarious position.

I fear Satan's ability to deceive is greater than most of us acknowledge. He is much better at pulling off the unexpected than most of us think. Because of our own experiences with failure we may comprehend this as individuals. Anyone who has been in a position of church leadership can also understand how all too often this plays itself out in congregational settings. But few realize how true his evil ambitions are regarding nations. For American Christians to fail to comprehend what is being revealed here would be an error of great magnitude. Nothing would please the enemy more than to deceive Christians and control the great assets of the United States of America.

2. In the end times Satan will give his authority to the beast described in Revelation 13.

We learn from the book of Job that the devil's authority over the world is limited by God's providential guidelines. Satan can only go so far. However, God's Word is clear that, on the whole, the systems developed by unregenerate man that make up society are controlled by Satan or under his influence. I John 5:19 states, "... that the whole world (or societies) is under the control of the evil one." It is why we're told not to love the world, be friends of the world, or be polluted by it (James 4:4, 1 John 2:15, James 1:27). It is why we're to put on the armor of God to oppose the powers of this dark world (Ephesians 6:10-12); and to no longer conform to the pattern of this world, but have our minds renewed, for then we will be able to test and approve what is God's will (Romans 12:2).

Jesus even acknowledged Satan's authority over the world when He was tempted by him.

> *The devil led him up to a high place and showed him in an instant all the kingdoms of the world. And he said to him, "I will give you all their authority and splendor, for it has been given to me, and I can give it to anyone I want to. So if you worship me, it will all be yours." (Luke 4:5-7)*

Satan claimed to have authority over the world, or society, and Jesus did not dispute his claim.

When we understand Satan's position of power and authority in the societies of this world, we can grasp John's statement in Revelation 13:2 about the devil investing this beast or superpower with his resources. For Satan to give "his power, his throne and great authority" to the beast would allow that superpower to assume the number-one position in all those elements that make up a society: military strength, politics, industry, economics, agriculture, production of goods and services, entertainment and so on. We know what country now holds this position in the world as these last days unfold.

So this beast is an extremely important figure that has awesome resources at its disposal. Revelation 13:4 states: "Men worshiped [held in awe] the dragon [Satan] because he had given authority to the beast, and they also worshipped the beast and asked, 'Who is like the beast? Who can make war against him?'"

Three verses later (verse 7), the text reads: "He [the beast or this superpower] was given power to make war against the saints and to conquer them. And he was given authority over every tribe, people, language and nation."

So the beast will be relentless in its warring against believers. It will use both methods Satan has relied on in his attacks: deception and persecution. <u>In fact, the time of testing Christians in America is already upon us.</u> The enemy's use of deception in this last generation has been stunning when you examine the rapid deterioration of our moral standards compared to biblical standards. I also think the enemy's use of deception is why Dr. Billy Graham found in his research, that over 90% of Christians in America are living defeated spiritual lives. When the time of outright persecution comes, will we handle it any better? This is an important question, because this future purge could obviously affect much of the U.S. population.

A Christian prisoner in Cuba was asked to sign a statement containing charges against fellow Christians that would lead to their arrest. He said, "The chains keep me from signing this." The Communist office protested, "But you are not in chains!" "I am," said the Christian. "I am bound by the chain of witnesses who, throughout the centuries, gave their lives for Jesus Christ. I am a link in this chain. I will not break it." [Source: Richard Wurmbrand: In the Face of Surrender: Over 200 Challenging and Inspiring Stories of Overcomers, copyright 1998.]

Because of our Christian heritage, Christians in America should expect to be in for some heavy spiritual battles as these last days unfold. Satan is out to destroy our country's strong spiritual base. I will say more about deception and persecution in Chapters 6 and 7.

Granted, we may never know for certain what or who this beast/superpower is until the events play themselves out. Even so, it seems the better part of wisdom to at least consider the possibilities. And if it is not the U.S., you can still be sure it will be the last great superpower.

3. This beast is a superpower, or possibly, an alliance of nations controlled by its dominant member.

This chapter is not long enough to develop this thought in detail. But even a cursory reading of the text gives the reader this impression. Here's chapter 13, verse 1(b): "He had ten horns and seven heads, with ten crowns on his horns, and on each head a blasphemous name."

Horns in Scripture are also kings, or the powers or nations they represent (see Revelation 17:12). So the bigger picture here is one of many powers aligned with the one dominate superpower.

The following discussion of this point is based on what I wrote in my longer book, *Salt & Light*.

Of all the identifying characteristics Scripture gives about the "beast" or superpower in Revelation 13, this one of having **"ten crowns on his horns"** is unique. <u>It is such a demanding and exacting description for any superpower to fulfill.</u> The word *crown* (some versions use *diadem*) was a distinctive mark of royalty among the early Greeks and Romans. If a country or nation is being discussed and the word *crown* or *diadem* is used, you know that something is being said about its political position.

We saw in the book of Daniel that the word *horns* is used in prophecy to refer to nations or countries. To add the word *crowns* with the descriptive word *horns* indicates this prophecy is referring to the political position of these *horns*, or nations, that the superpower in Revelation 13 influences.

Let me explain the phrase that describes this novel characteristic of the beast. The superpower has **"ten crowns on his horns"**, which prophetically describes how it could politically control various countries around the world, though it doesn't necessarily *exercise* control. The **crown is on the horn**, meaning political control rests with each individual country. When John says the crowns were positioned on the horns, he means each country has its own governing political body; the nations under the superpower's influence retain their autonomy.

If the superpower described in Revelation 13:1 politically controlled other countries, Scripture would have used the phrase "ten crowns on his <u>heads</u>," reflecting **the beast's political leadership** over each country. It would <u>not</u> have placed the crowns on the <u>horns</u>.

Notice how the Roman Empire in Revelation 12:3 is prophetically described. The *crowns* (political control) are on the *heads* (under Rome's control), not on the *horns* (individual countries under Roman rule were not allowed political autonomy).

I don't know of any superpower in history except the United States that has met this distinctive characteristic. For example, with our allies we defeated Germany and Japan in World War II, yet we allowed each country to retain political autonomy. We have not tried to rule them from Washington, D.C. Rather, we helped rebuild the countries we conquered. This prophetic imagery of crowns and horns, of politics and nations, is an accurate description of America's relationship with other powers. I know of no other nation that has ever had such a foreign policy.

Our influence stretches across the globe. The United States maintains more military bases and foreign embassies than any other power, and its technological, industrial and commercial influence pull even more of the world's peoples into its grasp. Missionaries journeying to faraway parts of the earth have found that American brand names, TV shows and popular music have preceded them. Yet none of these nations owe allegiance to the American flag. Not all that many under America's vast influence are actually citizens of the United States.

How aptly John's phrase of crowns and horns describes places that are heavily influenced by American culture and commerce but not ruled by American law and government.

4. This superpower and its leader are seen by some as interchangeable.

When in Revelation 13:4 the people ask, "Who can make war against <u>him</u>?", you may have noticed in some Bibles the use of the word "<u>him</u>" instead of "it." Some commentators feel the beast talked of here is the Antichrist. There is a sense in which this can be true. It was interesting to me, as a layman, to find my various translations of the Bible were equally divided between using the pronouns "him" and "it" when referring to the beast.

Therefore, for my own comfort level to make sure I was getting correct information, I acquired help from a seminary professor who has his doctorate in the Greek language. Were the pronouns "he," his" and "him" correct when referring to this beast in Revelation 13, which would indicate the beast refers to a man; or should the pronouns be "it" and "its", indicating the beast is a kingdom or superpower?

In Greek, the noun translated as "beast" in Revelation 13 is "*onpiov*." The word "*avrov*," also used in Revelation 13, is the pronoun that refers to the beast. To be grammatically correct, a pronoun must be of the same gender as the noun it refers to. If the original Greek word for "beast" is masculine gender, then the pronouns "he," "his" and "him" are the right translation; if it is neuter gender, then "it" and "its" are correct.

The Greek word for "beast" in Revelation 13 is neuter gender, meaning that "it" and "its" are the more exact translations. This is not a hypothetical answer but a grammatical fact. Bible publishers agree that to use the pronouns "he," "his" and "him"—the masculine gender—when referring to the beast is to use an incorrect translation of the pronoun (see *Greek-English New Testament*, Zondervan Publishing House, Grand Rapids, MI, 1975, p.751).

Let me repeat: The Greek word for "beast" is neuter. Therefore, the proper rendering of John's writing is to use the pronoun "it" and "its." This also means it is probable that John is using the word "beast" to refer to a superpower rather than to a man, as Daniel did. Granted, my position may not be held by all, as a nation and its leader can become synonymous. For example, a news headline that reads "BUSH CHALLENGES IRAN" could just as easily be "U.S. CHALLENGES IRAN."

It's a little like Nebuchadnezzar's dream in Daniel chapter 2. God's prophet tells the king that he (a man) is the golden head of the colossal statue. The next three parts of the great image—the chest and the arms, the belly and thighs, and the legs and feet—were kingdoms that would follow his. You can ask whether the head was King Nebuchadnezzar or his Babylonian kingdom. In the way Daniel was talking, the two were probably heard as one and the same.

The problem with placing too much emphasis in Revelation 13 on a person (the Antichrist), however, is that it takes away from thinking seriously about the identity of the superpower that will reign in these last days.

5. It is obvious to all that the beast has sustained a terrible injury of some sort.

Revelation 13:3 reads: "One of the heads of the beast seemed to have had a fatal wound, but the fatal wound had been healed." Please notice that only <u>one</u> of the beast's heads (the word "head" refers to a leadership position) received what appears to have been a fatal wound.

I'm sure by now you've figured out that in my thinking, this refers to the devastating defeat the U.S. military head (leadership) took at Pearl Harbor. I have already devoted the entire opening chapter to that catastrophic blow, so I won't go into it again. Suffice it to say that what the Axis powers saw as a strike of death to our military head, America not only recovered from, but that "wound" became the very springboard to her present position of phenomenal strength. That twist has to be more than mere coincidence.

Scripture states that the world is amazed at the beast's recovery. It is dramatic, awesome and inexplicable. We won a war on two fronts and ended the conflict with the dropping of the atomic bomb. Many nations then aligned themselves with our government and came under its influence. Our recovery catapulted the U.S.'s position of leadership over the earth. This new status as a superpower came about as a direct result of this recovery from a near-fatal blow.

The adult generation that felt firsthand the shockwaves of Pearl Harbor may be mostly removed from the present scene. But that doesn't in any way negate the magnitude of the event or the huge impact it had on our nation's future.

6. The reference to "blasphemous names" needs to be clearly understood.

Throughout the Old Testament, blasphemy was one of the gravest sins a person could commit. To blaspheme is to make light, or sport, of the name and sovereignty of God. In the New Testament, the Greek word for blasphemy means to injure one's reputation. The Scriptures are strict in teaching that the holy name of God is sacred. To misuse His name, either in normal conversation or in any way that is not marked with a sense of awe and majesty, is blasphemy.

It might help us understand the word *blasphemy* if we consider what happened prior to Christ's crucifixion. Jesus was true deity, but the Sanhedrin did not accept Him as such, so the high priest condemned Him to die for what this religious leader deemed blasphemy. The seriousness of this sin is shown by the fact that it was a capital offense. So when Jesus acknowledged His deity, the religious leaders claimed He had misused the name of God. This to them was blasphemy.

In describing the superpower in Revelation 13, when John speaks of the blasphemous name on each head, it means that the leadership of that government will misuse the sacred name of God. John indicates that in every facet of leadership, God's name will be used irreverently in carrying out what in reality are heinous acts.

As applied to the United States, this would mean our government promotes a worldly cause while at the same time claiming a special association with the God of the Bible. This is, in fact, what has happened in this last generation as our elected leaders began to pass laws that promote sin. Examples would be the condoning of sexual promiscuity in schools by passing out condoms, sponsoring the destruction of millions of unborn babies through abortion, and outlawing any reference to God in public schools, including praying out loud. There are numerous recent actions that our leaders have taken that have done serious damage to the name of God.

It would be bad enough if believers have seen the worst of these revisionist concepts. But you and I both know this is not the case. If we could look even 5, 10 or 15 years down the road, I think we'd be shocked by what the future holds for how we as a people think and act.

Undoubtedly, many of our nation's founders consciously submitted to the Lord's direction. But on our way to worldwide supremacy, later generations of Americans have abandoned that godly standard. It is true that other nations engage in wrongful activities, but few claim to have the blessing of the God of the Bible when their leaders commit such evils. And if they do, shame on them.

If this first verse of Revelation 13 was written in contemporary English, and the symbols were replaced with their contemporary explanations, it might read something like this:

> *I saw a world superpower develop in a new country made up of people of many nationalities. It profoundly influenced other powerful nations, holding a position of leadership in every aspect of world affairs. It did not try to politically rule these allies. Instead, they were allowed to govern themselves. This awesome empire used the name of God quite freely, albeit irreverently, while accomplishing its worldly activities.*

5

THE SECOND BEAST

Worship has long been Satan's desire. You recall him showing Jesus the kingdoms of the world and their splendor, then making Him this offer, "All this I will give you, if you will bow down and worship me."

"Worship" means to pay homage to, to attribute worth to, or to magnify the name of. A second beast in chapter 13 helps Satan and the first beast/superpower realize this long-held desire for adulation. Here is verse 12:

> *"Then I saw another beast, coming out of the earth. He had two horns like a lamb, but he spoke like a dragon."*

Earlier in the book of Revelation, Jesus was identified as the Lamb. Like a lamb, this second beast appears harmless, but it insidiously represents perverted values. In actuality, it is what Scripture calls a false prophet—pretending godliness, while at the same time undermining true spiritual values.

To whom is worship directed by this imposter lamb with horns? The next verse reads:

"He exercised all the authority of the first beast on his behalf, and made the earth and its inhabitants worship the first beast, whose fatal wound had been healed."

So the great pretender, Satan, now fashions his own religious rule. Please pay attention, however. It is not some kind of monstrosity. One of the literary devices we picked up as children was that bad things were pictured as hags and ogres. The good was portrayed by handsome princes and fair damsels. I'm concerned that by way of contrast, what will be presented to the curious by this spiritual charlatan will appear as quite an attractive package. The next verses read:

And he performed great and miraculous signs, even causing fire to come down from heaven to earth in full view of men. Because of the signs he was given power to do on behalf of the first beast, he deceived the inhabitants of the earth. He ordered them to set up an image in honor of the beast who was wounded by the sword (this indicates that the wound received by this superpower was a military wound) *and yet lived. He was given power to give breath to the image of the first beast, so that it could speak and cause all who refused to worship the image to be killed.*

Why killed? Because they refused to <u>worship</u> the image.

Throughout history, more often than not, religion and government have been strange bedfellows.

America was somewhat unique in its early declaration regarding the separation of church and state.

There is a problem with complete separation, however, or attempting to maintain a totally secular society where religion is isolated to certain worship hours in specific worship spaces. The difficulty is that this doesn't satisfy an innate need people have to interface 24/7 with something greater than the mere human.

Religion has great power. People are naturally curious about the supernatural and want it to touch their lives. Also, the more the worship is concrete or something physical, as opposed to spiritual, the better they seem to like it.

Satan would very much like to fill that void. But to try to do that frontally in a nation like America would still be extremely difficult. He almost has to come at this sideways. This way he won't prematurely call attention to what he is really about. To date, I believe the fruits of our society in this last generation reveals that he has kept his long-range intentions well-hidden through deception.

In the past, great empires and superpowers have relied on military might and political clout to dominate and control other countries. They would plunder the goods of the people and oftentimes tax them heavily. Even in modern times, communism ruled through the barrel of a gun. But the beast/superpower of Revelation 13 and its supporting cast employs a different power strategy to influence and dominate other peoples. It is far more subtle because of its spiritual facade. As miracles enhanced the ministry of Jesus, counterfeit or pseudo-miracles will mark the efforts of this second beast. In His Olivet Discourse, Jesus warned that "false Christs and false prophets will appear and perform great signs and miracles to deceive even the elect—if that were possible" (Matthew 24:24). People will view these wonders as the evidence of a new and wonderful religion and be drawn to it, not realizing they are being deceived. Apparently these recruitment tactics will be aided by technology.

Since World War II, our society's tremendous jump in world leadership has primarily been through the outgrowth of our advances in the electronic field. Most of these developments we now take for granted and consider commonplace. John writes about great and miraculous signs he saw, even fire coming down from heaven in full view of everyone. As a first-century man, this could be how he would be expected to describe some of our 21st-century marvels.

There is nothing inherently wrong with electricity or technology. It is a part of God's creation; electric power can be used in many wonderful ways including broadcasting Christian programs. But Satan controls the world; therefore, many of the marvels electricity makes possible are going to primarily be part of his system.

Television provides a direct means of mind control. It is a powerful influence that may appear harmless, but it often misleads through what it presents. Anything that has the ability to repetitively plant thoughts in our minds is a teacher and potential deceiver—a false prophet, so to speak.

The creation of electronic media in the last generation has allowed the devil to capture human imagination as never before. It has provided him a medium of teaching for every minute of every hour of every day. The notion hardly exists any more that there should be time and space reserved for family life. By far the largest exporter of TV programming, America impacts people around the world with our lifestyle, presenting our often-perverse values through the power of story.

John states that the combined political and secular influence of the second beast will fashion an "image" for the first beast. Since our main source of power has been developed through the technology of electronics, it would be logical that the image would be an electronic one. John writes that the second beast crafts an image of the first beast. The original Greek word he uses for "image" is "*eikon*," and it means "representation" or "manifestation." Revelation 13:17 says the image is used "so that no one could buy or sell unless he had the mark." John's language is not as incomprehensible as it appears. He is saying that there will be a product developed that gives government the ability through some means (the image) that it (the first beast) controls (by use of the mark) to monitor all the commercial activities (the buying and selling) of its citizens.

Consistent with the description given by John's prophecy, it appears this image has already been developed; more specifically, it is the electronic computer. No machine in history matches its influence. Since World War II, when America began to have dominance over the world, this amazing machine has become part of every facet of public and private life. Computers perform such an astonishing array of activities that modern life would be impossible without them. They possess a powerful technological brain—the microchip.

The entire world of commerce and industry now functions by use of computers. Transportation, from interstate trucking to airlines, relies on computers for everything from navigation to the scheduling of maintenance. Medicine, from diagnosing illness to filling prescriptions to cure them; department stores, banks, hospitals, utilities, post offices, churches, universities—nearly every modern institution functions by means of computer technology. The electronic computer is truly an image, or representation and manifestation, of a human creation using modern-day technology that fulfills John's prophecy. Some years ago, on January 3, 1983, *Time* magazine announced its "Man of the Year" was not a man at all, but the computer.

I don't know that much about computers. It is not difficult to see, however, that the harnessing of the earth's electromagnetic force of electricity, which was just lightning in the sky a few hundred years ago, has resulted in devices capable of performing complex human activities, including reproduction of the human voice. This fits John's references of the second beast's ability to make fire come down from heaven to earth and give breath to the image of the first beast, so that it could speak.

"He also forced everyone, small and great, rich and poor, free and slave, to receive a mark on his right hand or on his forehead, so that no one could buy or sell unless he had the mark" (Revelation 13:16-17a). Some day, yet to come, it will be necessary for the beast/superpower to control economic transactions. I don't know what all these commercial regulations will entail, but some kind of marking system will be imposed. At that time some supposed religious figures will no doubt assure their followers there is nothing to fear.

Did you know computers read marks, not numbers? A marking system of the kind John describes has already been developed. It can be found on practically every item on grocery shelves in retail stores. It is called the Universal Product Code (UPC), which looks like a series of vertical lines covering an area about the size of a large postage stamp. The UPC-symbol technology has been used in our country since 1973.

Although the bar codes on grocery items are the most noticeable, credit and bank cards also make use of barcodes. These are micro-encoded along the magnetic strip on the back of the card. When these marks are scanned by laser light, the optical pattern is converted to an electric signal (analog), which is converted in turn to a digital signal, then decoded by a microprocessor.

Literally tens of thousands of characters can be micro-encoded on the 3" × 0.5" magnetic strip on a single card. It is possible to record a personal record of every person's purchases, transactions, and so on.

This kind of record-keeping already takes place in business for anyone who orders merchandise through a company like Amazon.com. When you sign in to your account, the site offers you a list of items it has selected for you to consider based on your previous purchases. Amazon not only keeps track of what you have bought in the past, but for the duration of each online session it tracks what items you have viewed. After you place an item into your electronic shopping cart, Amazon.com gives you a list of items that other shoppers bought at the same time they bought the item you've just purchased.

The question is always asked, when do I think this system of economic control will unfold? That I don't know! The technology for a cashless society already exists. Credit cards make the introduction of a national identification card possible right now. In addition, existing technology could be used to implant information beneath the skin on the head, arm or other body parts. And new technology is constantly being introduced. The manipulation for using such technology for social control might follow a major social or political event, appear in the aftermath of a natural disaster, or result from the fallout of a major economic shake-up.

I am not an economics whiz, but it is not difficult to understand why many economists are warning that the heavy debt we have incurred over the past 15-20 years will someday have to be paid back. For some, this heavy debt is a matter of greed. These people already have more than most everyone else in the world, yet they are still not satisfied. For most Americans, however, heavy indebtedness is a matter of ignoring economic reality. We have grown accustomed to the material possessions that make up what we call "the good life," and few seem to realize that they have become victims of a worldly deception that ensnares people through irresistible advertising and product availability.

We have been led to expect a lifestyle that is getting harder and harder to achieve. Therefore, the widening gap between expectations and capabilities has created a nearly irresistible dependence on credit. Buying on credit is the only way for many Americans to get what we now think of as our birthright. Few understand the reality of our nation's economic position in comparison to the rest of the world. We have fallen into heavy debt. Personal debt has reached a record high; savings, an all-time low. Government is in the same boat. Cities, states and the federal government must borrow in order to maintain public services. Credit has put a stranglehold on our economy.

As a result, we have dug ourselves into an economic hole. During the 1980s, our country went from being the largest creditor nation in the world to the largest debtor nation. People face huge personal debt. Corporations juggle massive business debt. Government operates with colossal deficits.

Few politicians and corporate chieftains seem willing to admit this, but our years of unconscious overspending cannot be eradicated. No matter what the politicians promise, record indebtedness could ultimately result in financial judgment.

In a larger sense, what the government does or doesn't do at this point won't make much difference. Current "solutions" to the debt crisis amount to economic fiction rather than sound economic thinking. Take the idea of consumer spending. The notion is that the economy will be healthy as long as consumer spending remains strong. In other words, everybody will be poorer unless people spend more than they can afford. That just doesn't make sense!

Many economists predict there is no way to spend our way out of this economic dilemma—that is the real "bottom line." Whether consumers spend more, or spend less; whether the government taxes more, or taxes less, the debt will continue to grow. Traditional methods taken to prop up the economy simply are not feasible. No conventional solutions are available because this is an unheard-of economic problem.

The "spirit of merchandising" has grabbed people's hearts, and many American families now depend on two incomes to meet their debt obligations. The loss of one income even for a brief period would tilt them dangerously close to financial ruin. At the root of this economic vulnerability is our failure to live within our means. Consumer debt, mortgage debt, government debt, plus corporate debt has risen in a vain effort to maintain our present standard of living. <u>We have mortgaged the future to pay for the present.</u>

At some stage, we will reach that critical point where the rising debt collides with falling earnings. When the right portion of debt goes unpaid, the credit system that drives our economy will falter. What will break the camel's back—the shock that will trigger a major economic change—is unknown.

I believe there could be significant social and political fallout to a major economic catastrophe. An extreme money panic might bring civil disorder, violence and unimaginable chaos, not necessarily because Americans will lack basic necessities, but because we will be denied the things we want.

This is not the same as it was in our country during the Great Depression. During the 1930s, the majority of people were accustomed to working hard for simple necessities. The generation that survived the Depression was glad to have enough to eat, something to wear, and a roof over their heads. But our self-centered, materialistic, technology-dependent generation will not be content with that.

If this should happen, few Americans will resist government intervention; in fact, many will probably demand it. This will open the door that will give future leaders great incentive to eliminate perceived threats to the economy by exerting direct control over buying and selling. It could be a simple matter for the leaders of the beast-system to promise social order in return for absolute compliance.

It is difficult to say in detail what these commercial regulations will entail, but Bible prophecy clearly points to that day when a superpower will control economic transactions. A marking system of some kind will be imposed as John prophesied. As stated earlier, a computer reads "marks," not numbers. Only by the foreknowledge of God could John have known this.

What will be the response of multitudes of people to this miracle-worker who finally brings order out of chaos? The answer is that most people will be thrilled by the miracles performed. They will welcome this as nothing less supernatural. Most will be far more compliant than anyone imagines. They will cheer this problem-solver, in fact, even willingly yield to the system of this beast/superpower with an attitude of worship. Its edicts they will follow and the general public will indeed be most happy once again. "Who is like our savior?" they will claim.

Again, worship means to pay homage to, to attribute worth to, or to magnify the name of. How pleased the enemy and his followers will be when this finally happens. The forces of darkness have long waited for this day to dawn. Worldwide reverence has evaded them for ever so long.

It doesn't matter if they compose new hymns and sing them in the beast's honor, as long as it has their heartfelt commitment. If its name is spontaneously extolled in praise will probably be more satisfying to this beast/superpower than small-town robed choirs each week rehearsing special numbers when they wouldn't be heard anyway.

The worship may not be the same as what we have known in our churches. But it will be there nevertheless. Television will be a part of it. So will magazines, books, newspapers and the Internet. Great rallies will resound with the beast's praises. Schoolchildren will be taught how intelligent the beast is. Its glory will be inferred in the movies. And organized religion will once again be its bed partner.

A scapegoat will be made of any who dare oppose this new "superpower." That discomforting thought prepares you for the next two chapters, which were written to help you to be ready for just such a time.

6

Patient Endurance and Faithfulness

No one likes being blindsided.

Fights are bad enough to begin with. Hitting someone when they aren't expecting it is the way cowards do things.

Part of the reason Americans were so enraged in their response to Pearl Harbor was that at the very time the Japanese planes were completing their mission, two envoys from Tokyo were carrying on the pretense of diplomatic negotiations with the U.S. Secretary of State, Cordell Hull.

To make certain Satan will not catch His people by surprise, Jesus gave John a message that informed them about what to expect. What He said was not always comforting, but the bottom line was that He would be triumphant, and faithfulness to Him would be rewarded.

> *But the beast was captured, and with him the false*
> *prophet who had performed the miraculous signs*

on his behalf. With these signs he had deluded those who had received the mark of the beast and worshiped his image. The two of them were thrown alive into the fiery lake of burning sulfur. (Revelation 19:20)

And I saw an angel coming down out of heaven, having the key to the Abyss and holding in his hand a great chain. He seized the dragon, that ancient serpent, who is the devil, or Satan, and bound him for a thousand years. (Revelation 20:1-2)

And I saw the souls of those who had been beheaded because of their testimony for Jesus and because of the word of God. They had not worshiped the beast or his image and had not received his mark on their foreheads or their hands. They came to life and reigned with Christ a thousand years. (Revelation 20:4)

That's the good news. The bad news is that before these positive events take place, there is a time of terrible persecution. In His Olivet Discourse, Jesus says:

Those will be days of distress unequaled from the beginning, when God created the world, until now—and never to be equaled again. If the Lord had not cut short those days, no one would survive. But for the sake of the elect, whom he has chosen, he has shortened them." (Mark 13:19-20)

The picture presented in Revelation 13 includes a time of persecution. Here are verses 5-8:

The beast was given a mouth to utter proud words and blasphemies and to exercise his authority for

forty-two months. He opened his mouth to blaspheme
God, and to slander his name and his dwelling place
and those who live in heaven. He was given power
to make war against the saints and to conquer them.
And he was given authority over every tribe, people,
language and nation. All inhabitants of the earth will
worship the beast—all whose names have not been
written in the book of life belonging to the Lamb that
was slain from the creation of the world.

Both in the past and in the present, Christians have experienced terrible times of suffering for their faith. But for some, at least, there was always the hope of escape to another country. For example, in 1977, Anglican Bishop Festo Kivengere of Uganda was urged by his people to flee the country following the murder of Archbishop Janani Luwum by the forces of dictator Idi Amin. The believers told Festo and his wife, "One bishop's death this weekend is enough for us." Under the cover of night, the two made it on foot across a mountain pass to Rwanda. But in the book of Revelation, Jesus lets us know that a day will come when there will no longer be a place to which His people can flee. That's because the beast will be in authority over "every tribe, people, language and nation."

Back in 1986, a powerful movie came out called *The Mission* starring Jeremy Irons. He plays a Spanish Jesuit who goes to South America in the early years of colonization to convert the Indians. His loving efforts prove quite successful, and he builds a remarkable mission that greatly enhances the lives of the natives. Robert De Niro also gives a strong performance as a

slave-hunter who, surprisingly, is converted and sub-
sequently helps in this ministry. Conflict is introduced
when Spain sells the territory to her neighbor Portugal.
The question naturally arises as to what will happen to
the mission, and should it be defended against the Por-
tuguese aggressors. De Niro's character opts to take up
arms. The Jesuit father, just as strong in his own beliefs,
says no, and is willing to sacrificially lay down his life
if need be. The movie doesn't side with either of the
difficult options. It lets the story tell itself. The viewer
is left to consider which was the better choice.

The persecution referred to in Revelation 13 is
carried out under the providence of God, and therefore
any kind of armed resistance will be out of the question.
There is to be no taking up of weapons and fighting
back. That's the reason for the words of Revelation
13:10, which reads: "If anyone is to go into captivity,
into captivity he will go. If anyone is to be killed with
the sword, with the sword he will be killed."

Although the verse doesn't include the word
"martyrdom," it is certainly another possibility. Martyrs are an integral part of the book of Revelation. For
example, chapter 6, verses 9-11 reads:

> *When he opened the fifth seal, I saw under the altar
> the souls of those who had been slain because of
> the word of God and the testimony they had main-
> tained. They called out in a loud voice, "How long,
> Sovereign Lord, holy and true, until you judge the
> inhabitants of the earth and avenge our blood?"
> Then each of them was given a white robe, and they
> were told to wait a little longer, until the number of*

their fellow servants and brothers who were to be killed as they had been was completed.

Here's chapter 7, verses 13-17:

Then one of the elders asked me, "These in white robes—who are they, and where did they come from?" I answered, "Sir, you know." And he said, "These are they who have come out of the great tribulation; they have washed their robes and made them white in the blood of the Lamb. Therefore, they are before the throne of God and serve him day and night in his temple; and he who sits on the throne will spread his tent over them. Never again will they hunger; never again will they thirst. The sun will not beat upon them, nor any scorching heat. For the Lamb at the center of the throne will be their shepherd; he will lead them to springs of living water. And God will wipe away every tear from their eyes."

And Revelation 12, verse 11:

"They overcame him (Satan) by the blood of the Lamb and by the word of their testimony; they did not love their lives so much as to shrink from death."

The church has always flourished during times when Christians have bravely chosen death rather than to deny their faith. The assumption, therefore, is that this future worldwide testimony of countless martyrs will also, for the first time in history, bring about a revival in all countries of the globe. Key to what happens will not be biblical preaching, but rather the silent suffering of the saints.

What will sustain the faithful won't be sermons they recall about the Prosperity Gospel, but rather those teachings they were given about being faithful even during desperately hard times. It's Bible stories like Shadrach, Meshach and Abednego in Daniel chapter 3 saying to the king in verses 17 and 18,

> *"If we are thrown into the blazing furnace, the God we serve is able to save us from it, and he will rescue us from your hand, O king. But even if he does not, we want you to know, O king, that we will not serve your gods or worship the image of gold you have set up."*

Bible passages hidden in believers' hearts will be deeply appreciated. I'm referring to verses about faithfulness, like:

> *Praise be to the LORD, for he showed his wonderful love to me. ... You heard my cry for mercy when I called to you for help. Love the LORD, all his saints! The LORD preserves the faithful. ... Be strong and take heart, all you who hope in the LORD. (Psalm 31:21-24)*

> *Do not be afraid of what you are about to suffer. I tell you, the devil will put some of you in prison to test you, and you will suffer persecution. ... Be faithful, even to the point of death, and I will give you the crown of life. (Revelation 2:10)*

> *But the fruit of the Spirit is love, joy, peace, patience, kindness, goodness, faithfulness, gentleness and self-control. (Galatians 5:22-23a)*

The living, the living—they praise you, as I am doing today; <u>fathers tell their children about your faithfulness.</u> (Isaiah 38:19)

Of course the Revelation 13:10 verse that ends this paragraph about the war the beast makes on the saints concludes: "This calls for patient endurance and faithfulness on the part of the saints." So it's faithfulness and patient endurance.

Verses about patient endurance that come to mind include:

Rather, as servants of God we commend ourselves in every way: <u>in great endurance</u>; in troubles, hardships and distresses; in beatings, imprisonments and riots; in hard work, sleepless nights and hunger…

That's Paul in 2 Corinthians 6:4-5. An even more powerful example is found in Hebrews 12:2 and 3…

Let us fix our eyes on Jesus, the author and perfecter of our faith, who for the joy set before him <u>endured</u> the cross, scorning its shame, and sat down at the right hand of the throne of God. Consider him who <u>endured</u> such opposition from sinful men, so that you will not grow weary and lose heart.

As this generation of Americans has continued to be blessed with freedom and peace, brothers and sisters in Christ the world over have had to practice patient endurance and faithfulness. One illustration is hardly adequate to represent the whole, but let's return momentarily to Uganda, where the East African revival has been going on for decades.

Archbishop Janani Luwam will always be a hero to believers there. For his opposition to dictator Idi Amin, Luwam was imprisoned on charges that he was hiding weapons for an armed rebellion. The church knew this was false because it had affirmed from the beginning that it would never be involved in using force or weapons. Their belief was that evil had to be overcome by good.

In his book *Revolutionary Love*, Bishop Festo Kivengere (mentioned earlier in this chapter) describes the scene:

> *More than four thousand people walked, unintimidated, past Idi Amin's guards to pack St. Paul's Cathedral in Kampala on February 20. They repeatedly sang the "Martyrs' Song," which had been sung by the young Ugandan martyrs in 1885. Those young lads had only recently come to know the Lord, but they loved Him so much that they could refuse the evil things demanded of them by King Mwanga. They died in the flames singing, "Oh that I had wings such as angels have, I would fly away to be with the Lord." They were given wings, and the singing of those thousands at the Memorial Service had wings too.*
>
> *We have no way of estimating the fresh impetus given by the martyrdom of Luwum to the Body of Christ. In Heaven we will know. After the service in the cathedral, the crowd gathered outside around the little cemetery where a grave had been dug for Janani beside that of Bishop Hannington, the first bishop for Central Africa sent out from England to*

*the young church in Uganda. He was martyred by
the same king in the same year as the boys.*

*Our archbishop's grave was empty because we had
been denied the body of our leader. Soldiers had
taken it far north to his own village of Kitgum for
burial, in order to avoid the embarrassment to Amin
of the discovery that he had died by bullets, not by
a car accident as was pretended. At the open grave,
former Archbishop Erica Sabiti quoted the words of
the angels at the empty tomb of Jesus, "He is not
here, He is risen!" Instantly a song of Zion burst out
with such power that "Glory, glory, hallelujah" was
heard from that hilltop far into the city. (77-78)*

The number of Christian martyrs throughout the
world during the 1900s, as estimated by David B. Bar-
rett and his colleagues, was 45,400,000. Since 1950
there have been 13,300,000 Christians martyred, and
since A.D. 33, the total is estimated to be 69,420,000.
(Source: *World Christian Encyclopedia*, Global Dia-
gram 6)

Patient endurance and faithfulness will be called
for again when persecution is the order of the day
everywhere throughout the world. The big question is
whether American believers will be prepared to stand
with their brothers and sisters from such places as
Afghanistan, Algeria, Azerbaijan, Bangladesh, Bhu-
tan, China, Colombia, Cuba, Egypt, Ethiopia, India,
Indonesia, Iran, Iraq, Laos, Libya, Morocco, Myanmar
(Burma), Nepal, Nigeria, North Korea, Pakistan, Qa-
tar, Saudi Arabia, Somalia, Sri Lanka, Sudan, Syria,

Tajikistan, Tibet, Tunisia, Turkey, Turkmenistan, Uzbekistan, Vietnam, Yemen and still more nations where Christians are already frequently persecuted.

The ministry "The Voice of the Martyrs" says this year an estimated 160,000 Christians will die at the hands of their oppressors, and more than 200 million will be arrested, tortured, beaten or jailed. That's equal to 2/3 of the present United States population. Did you know that in many countries it is illegal to own a Bible, share your faith, change your faith or allow children under 18 to attend a religious service?

This is in spite of the fact that the United Nations' "Universal Declaration of Human Rights," Article 10, reads:

> *Everyone has the right to freedom of thought, conscience and religion; this right includes freedom to change his religion or belief, and freedom, either alone or in community with others and in public or private, to manifest his religion or belief in teaching, practice, worship and observance.*

Most American Christians would agree that faithfulness and patient endurance are good qualities. In real life, however, people tend to resist being trained in these areas. Patient endurance means sticking in there even when the going gets tough. It often requires bearing with pain or injury without yielding, tolerating suffering with fortitude.

Faithfulness has to do with being trustworthy in the performance of duty, standing by your promises or obligations. 1 Corinthians 4:2 reads: "Now it is required that those who have been given a trust must prove faithful."

In this country, people's attitudes tend to be more that of, "I don't need this hassle. Treat me nice or I'm out of here."

Often it's how they relate to God too. "You have had more than enough time, Lord, to answer my prayers. If you don't meet my needs, why should I stick with you?"

The truth is, patient endurance and faithfulness are not lessons we're all that fond of, which doesn't bode well in terms of us being prepared for future hardships.

Here is a simple prayer that could serve us well in terms of preparing for the days ahead.

Lord,

I give you permission to start teaching me about patient endurance and faithfulness. I know I am not as skilled in these matters as I should be. When you sense I have started to learn these lessons, I pray that you would also help me share them with those I love the most.

Amen

The time will come when justice and fair-mindedness is set aside for the will of tyrants and Jesus-haters. This ill treatment will not be something new. The world has already had more than its share of abuse of this kind. The only difference will be in its scope. It will encompass the entire globe.

It will do no good to look to the courts to make things right. They will be under the control of the beast/superpower. The same will be true of the police and the military. The nightmare will be complete because, as impossible as it sounds, even some of the religious authorities will answer to it.

Christians will be treated like outcasts, those despised by all. Justice for them will be a joke. To look for mercy will be an exercise in futility. It will not be found. It will be a time of great misery and sorrow.

But it won't last all that long.

In His time the rightful King will return in triumph. Rev. 21:1-4 …

> *Then I saw a new heaven and a new earth, for the first heaven and the first earth had passed away, and there was no longer any sea.*
>
> *I saw the Holy City, the new Jerusalem, coming down out of heaven from God, prepared as a bride beautifully dressed for her husband. And I heard a loud voice from the throne saying, "Now the dwelling of God is with men, and he will live with them. They will be his people, and God himself will be with them and be their God. He will wipe every tear from their eyes. There will be no more death or mourning or crying or pain, for the old order of things has passed away."*

7

THE ENEMY'S ATTACK METHODS

Since WWII the Lord has allowed the beast/superpower to use deception as a powerful weapon to test our commitment to obedience. Possibly the best way for me to illustrate this for you is to refer to an example from my birth family.

My brother Dr. Charles Fraley, M.D., now retired, spent 30 productive years as a medical missionary in Kenya, East Africa with Africa Inland Mission. He was the executive director of a ministry overseeing the work of five hospitals, more than 50 health clinics across the country, and a nursing school. His responsibilities were endless. He performed surgery, assisted in administration, taught staff members, checked on patients, delivered supplies, and worked with the Kenyan government to obtain licenses for long-and short-term doctors and nurses coming into the country. He was the attending physician for missionaries from all denominations. Many of his days were spent traversing rock, dirt and sand roads and paths, traveling among the African tribes while avoiding potentially deadly wild animals and thieves.

Before going to the mission field, however, my brother had a dramatic experience that I believe illustrates what all too often happens to present-day American Christians.

Charles had been dedicated to Christ from his youth. Upon graduating from high school he entered the Navy. He had considerable spare time while on ship duty and spent those hours learning the Word of God. His normal routine was to rise two hours before wakeup call to pray, study the Word and memorize verses.

After military service he entered Bible College in Nyack, New York, on the G.I. Bill. One evening, while he was asking the Lord for guidance, his prayer was quickly followed by a vision. He saw a man straddling the ocean with one foot in Africa and the other in America. This person, dressed in doctor's clothing, was saying, *"Come over and help, come over and help."* Dr. Fraley felt honored that this call was similar to the Macedonian vision that the Apostle Paul experienced.

As he sought the precise meaning, the Spirit of the Lord rose in his being in a strong way, convincing him that he was to become a doctor and go to Africa to minister to the poor and needy.

Charles then transferred to Taylor University in Upland, Indiana, where he completed his premedical schooling. From there it was off to Ohio State University for four years, leading up to his graduation from medical school. He next served one year of internship and four years of surgical residency at Saint Elisabeth Hospital in Youngstown, Ohio. So he invested 13 years of his life preparing to be obedient to the Lord's call to go to Africa as a missionary doctor.

But something unexpected happened during those long years of preparation. Somehow he slipped in his spiritual commitment and lost sight of his original goal. The enemy subtly put the thought in his mind that he could serve the Lord just as effectively by practicing medicine in the States. He reasoned that this would allow him, along with his wife Marlene and their two children, to enjoy at least some of the benefits available to doctors in this country. Friends in the medical profession and other believers agreed. Besides, if he wanted someday to go to Africa, it would be good to have some stateside experience. Dr. Fraley admits he was rationalizing at that point, because the truth is he had received a powerful summons from the Lord as to what he should do.

In the early 1970s Dr. Fraley's medical practice in the States flourished. Soon he was earning an annual income of $300,000-plus. His family was able to buy just about anything they wanted.

It seemed life couldn't be better. He would say that, materially speaking, this was true. He hardly realized that the enemy had used the influence of America's comfortable surroundings to cause him to disobey divine direction. By setting up a medical practice in the States, he had gone against what the Lord wanted.

He was quite obviously walking away from God's will for him.

Being out of sync with heaven's plan seemed to quickly open other ways for the enemy to tempt this good man, resulting in him falling prey to an even greater deception. It happened about four years after he started his medical practice. In consideration of others, he does not share details, except to say that his actions were definitely not in agreement with the Word of God. The truth is, he was on a path that had the potential to destroy everything he held dear, including his family. Of course, this was what Satan wanted! Like Eve was deceived to eat the fruit from the Garden, Charles says, "The enemy deceived me."

Please understand that Dr. Fraley had been active in church all during this time. He still studied the Word and spent time in prayer, but he wasn't thinking as clearly as he should have been. Compromise had clouded his spiritual perception. DECEPTION BREEDS COMPROMISE, WHICH LEADS TO DISOBEDIENCE AND SPIRITUAL DEFEAT!

Fortunately, the Lord used another Christian to lift the veil from Dr. Fraley's spiritual eyes. His testimony is evidence of the importance of other believers in our lives. It recalls King David and how the Lord used Nathan to open his eyes after he had fallen into deception.

Realizing that he was not walking in conformity to God's will was devastating to Charles. His waywardness crushed his spirit! This caused him to seek the

Lord with all the strength he had, and with a heart of true repentance. His path to victory included not only contrition for his sin, but a willingness to retrace his steps to where things had gone wrong and a return to his original call of missionary doctoring in Africa. For seven months, every ounce of his being was exerted in seeking God through prayer, meditation and worship. He mostly wanted to know how this could have happened, and why so many fellow Christians seem to be living defeated lives.

At the end of this period, he and his family went away on a two-week vacation. Much of his time was still spent in prayer. Midway through the second week he had another vision. It was similar to the one through which the Lord called him to missionary work. The new vision was that of a large head of a beast—huge and menacing—hovering over America. It was swallowing Christians—scores of them in a brief period of time—almost at will. It was a horrifying and chilling picture, as you can well imagine.

The Spirit of the Lord showed Dr. Fraley the meaning of this remarkable revelation. This beast represented the materialistic and pleasure-seeking lifestyle that is so common throughout the land, even among church people. Its influence is so powerful it causes otherwise-strong believers to lose their spiritual edge. This is why so many have become apathetic about the deterioration of biblical standards the majority of Americans lived by until recently, and why thousands of Christian families are experiencing spiritual defeat.

Christians who were being overcome were not aware of what was happening. It was how Dr. Fraley had been deceived and overcome in his spiritual walk.

The previous chapter revealed how Satan also desires to use persecution to war against end-time Christians. Until persecution can be implemented in America, the major method the devil is utilizing is deception. Scripture and church history record numerous examples of both persecution and deception. My brother's experience is an illustration of what I believe has been happening on a massive scale. Granted, most people are not called to be medical missionaries to Africa, but too many have missed altogether what God wills for their lives and are being greatly influenced by the ungodly standards of our society, resulting in their walking in disobedience to God's Word.

SATANIC DECEPTION

For whatever reason, this diabolical strategy all too often goes undetected. Therefore, Christians go about living their lives unprotected, which allows them to be overcome almost at the devil's every whim.

There is one sure way to determine the presence of deception. It is by an examination of the fruit produced. In Chapter 2, I looked briefly at some of the fruit produced in our society since the end of World War II. That is the kind of examination we must regularly make if we want to know how successful the enemy has been at using spiritual deception to overcome believers. Keep in mind that …

> *The fruit of the Spirit is love, joy, peace, patience, kindness, goodness, faithfulness, gentleness and self-control. ... Since we live by the Spirit, let us keep in step with the Spirit. Let us not become conceited, provoking and envying each other. (Galatians 5:22, 25-26)*

Spiritual deception has caused the world's influence on Christians in this generation to be greater than the influence we have on the world. That was not generally true in America until this last generation.

One of Scripture's strongest warnings concerning spiritual deception in the last days came from Jesus. What He said deals with the type of deception that caused Dr. Fraley to fall, and it is causing many other Christians to fail. Jesus cautioned:

> *"Just as it was in the days of Noah, so also will it be in the days of the Son of Man. People were eating, drinking, marrying and being given in marriage up to the day Noah entered the ark." Then the flood came and destroyed them all. It was the same in the days of Lot. People were eating and drinking, buying and selling, planting and building. But the day Lot left Sodom, fire and sulfur rained down from heaven and destroyed them all. (Luke 17:26-29)*

Jesus does not mention the gross sins that were taking place in Noah's day, which is what we usually hear about when this passage is discussed. In fact, not one of the things He brings up is thought of as a sin. His comparison is with the everyday busyness of people: drinking, eating, marrying, buying, selling, planting and building.

Why does He talk about these routine matters of life? I believe the answer goes to the heart of the spiritual deception now taking place in our country. Jesus gave us this prophetic warning because He knew one of the primary concerns of Christians living in our day would be their <u>over-commitment</u> to the normal activities of life—the eating, drinking, buying, selling, building, and so on. Our sin is the giving of our hearts to self-serving aspects of life, over and above our commitment to live by God's standards. *"Where shall we eat tonight?" "What shall we do on the weekend?" "Should we sell this house and get a bigger one in a better neighborhood?"* That kind of thing happened in the days of Noah, and it is happening again today in America. This fatal flaw prevented the people in Noah's day from paying attention to the signs of the times, and the identical clouded thinking is taking its toll on today's society. Our fruit reveals this truth!

Dr. Fraley's testimony is a wonderful witness to the mercy of God. He repented and sought the Lord to once again walk in His will and in the fullness of His Spirit. Not only did God restore him, but the fruit the Lord produced through him during the 30 years he spent on the mission field was remarkable. I know because I have been to Kenya, East Africa. I have talked with the people there and have seen with my own eyes all that was accomplished.

NATIONAL APPLICATION

When examining the spiritual development of America, it's obvious to me that God has a special place in His heart, and a special calling, for America. Human wisdom alone did not develop our country. Men inspired by God were at the core of every aspect of our nation's early development. I find that, except for Israel, God has never intervened in a country's spiritual development as much as He has in America.

The Lord has a special calling for America in these days also. I believe His mission for these end times is for us to be the "salt of the earth" and the "light of the world." Unfortunately, as he deceived Dr. Fraley, the enemy has deceived the American church community over the last 40-50 years, and our fruit reveals that we have fallen away from our calling, leaving our nation spiritually unprotected. But as my brother testifies, he was restored and experienced a personal revival, and he fulfilled his original commitment. I am convinced that this principle can also apply to the church in America. There is a lot of discussion about revival in the body of Christ, but for this to happen it will certainly take a spirit of repentance and turning from the ways of the world.

God's Word gives us the formula for national revival in 2 Chronicles 7:14. He says:

> *"If my people, who are called by my name, will humble themselves and pray and seek my face and turn from their wicked ways, then I will hear from heaven and forgive their sins and will heal their land."*

This is exactly the pattern followed by Dr. Fraley. He humbled himself, sought the face of the Lord, repented and turned from the sin in which he was involved, and the Lord spiritually healed him. Please notice this verse states "if my people." It is the people of God who must follow these instructions. It is not a calling to the people of the world.

If we as Christians are willing to humble ourselves, pray, seek the Lord's face, and renounce the ways of the world that lead us astray, the Lord will surely restore America's Christian heritage and our calling for these last days.

PERSONAL RESPONSE

Christians need to wake up to Satan's deceptive strategy regarding America. Even if the churches of this land fail to know another season of glorious revival, individual believers would be wise to make certain their lives are in line with what God expects of them. Like Noah of old, having been alerted about what lies ahead, we need to respond appropriately. Hebrews 11:7 reads: "By faith Noah, when warned about things not yet seen, <u>in holy fear built an ark to save his family.</u>"

Holy fear is what motivates us to live by God's standards, and to not give into worldly preoccupations and pressures. Believing the warning I received about America becoming the superpower of Revelation 13 <u>put within me a holy fear in my walk with the Lord.</u>

To have a holy fear is to stand in awe of Him and to have a deep respect for His desires. Possession of this characteristic is what gives us the inner desire to avoid anything and everything that might displease God. Instead, obedience to the Lord becomes our top priority.

Holy fear develops the desire to subject our lives to one exacting standard: "Is this pleasing to the Lord?" Therefore, holy fear develops a heart that is always open to correction and repentance.

Christians who have a proper fear of the Lord have nothing to be afraid of in the days to come, no matter what happens. Great courage against the enemy begins with a holy fear of God.

> *"Learn to fear the LORD your God…" (Deuteronomy 31:12)*

> *"The LORD confides in those who fear him." (Psalm 25:14)*

> *"But the eyes of the LORD are on those who fear him." (Psalm 33:18)*

> *"The angel of the LORD encamps around those who fear him, and he delivers them." (Psalm 34:7)*

> *"For those who fear him lack nothing." (Psalm 34:9)*

> *"Through the fear of the LORD a man avoids evil." (Proverbs 16:6)*

> *"He who fears the LORD has a secure fortress, and for his children it will be a refuge." (Proverbs 14:26)*

"Then the church ... was strengthened; and encouraged by the Holy Spirit ... living in the fear of the LORD." (Acts 9:31)

"Live your lives as strangers here in reverent fear." (1 Peter 1:17)

A word the Lord gave me for living in these last days was, "Fear not the days to come, but fear this only: That you shall walk in a manner pleasing to the Lord."

It is most unfortunate that godly fear no longer characterizes America. In many ways it has disappeared from the church as well. In a world not that unlike our own, Noah stood out as being different. The verse reads that he "in holy fear built an ark to save his family." Putting obedience to what God told him above everything else in life, he prepared his family for events that would mean the destruction of ever so many others. I believe this same attitude is what will drive behaviors that will protect families that choose to live decidedly Christian in today's world. It's what I call "building spiritual arks of safety."

SPIRITUAL ARKS OF SAFETY

By "building spiritual arks of safety" I don't mean withdrawing from the world. Scripture tells us we are to be in the world, but not of it. What I have in mind is protecting those we love by doing everything within our power to see to it that obedience to the Lord is their number-one priority.

I went so far as to write down what that looks like for my wife Barbara and me in the book *Salt and*

Light: Subtitle, *Fulfilling God's Mission for America in these Last Days.* Even if I were to suddenly die, my loved ones would still know what I believe and how that has shown itself in my life. The book makes this plain. It's what we have come to embrace through over four decades of following Christ together. If anyone wants to know what the two of us are passionate about in our Christian walk, it's there in the book.

Your experience will likely differ from ours. I have no doubt but that in some ways you will have passed us spiritually in what you have learned. We sincerely want to hear what God has taught you. Even today, how are you preparing for the future? Testimonies from people like you are what we see as an integral part of Campaign Save Christian America. This Web site (www.campaignsaveamerica.com) is a place where we can learn from one another how God is growing us in our faith, especially in these days when it appears that the coming of the Lord is not that far off.

This Web site has a number of features. But the one that probably interests me the most is where people can read how others are preparing for those closest to them to be able to stand strong in both the world of today and the world of tomorrow. That's what "spiritual arks of safety" are about.

Here is an example of what one person shared:

At our church I was challenged to write out a list of my present and 5 and 10 year prayer requests for the people I love the most. This assignment changed my prayer life from what I now realize was a somewhat superficial approach to one of becoming a real prayer warrior on behalf of my family and close friends. This single exercise also got me started in keeping a prayer notebook, which has had a profound effect on my walk with the Lord. Writing my prayers, even as elementary as the form I use is, has brought alive my times with the Lord, and given me a deeper love than I ever could have imagined for those I pray for.

I am in my seventies. My two eyes are not as strong as they used to be. My spiritual sight, though, has been improving with age. I see the beast of Revelation 13 more clearly than I did when I was at my prime, physically speaking.

Though I have not had a vision like my brother did, in my mind I can easily envision the beast he told me about. It's gruesome and grotesque and continues to feed on believers as it sits astride our nation. I am passionate in my desire to destroy it. Because that is a bigger job than I can accomplish on my own, I do all within my power to make people aware of its diabolical presence.

All this could result in living with an ongoing nightmare, were it not for the fact that my eyes are really fixed on Jesus. His presence is quite real to me. He fills my days in such a way that my focus is completely on Him.

The truth is, I am an aging and contented Christian gentleman to whom the Lord has been remarkably gracious. What I am most thankful to Him for is that all those in my immediate family love and serve Him.

They are in our "spiritual ark of safety." Thank you Jesus!

I hope that what I have written about America and her future is wrong. But ever since the Lord inspired me to explore this possibility over 35 years ago, there is nothing in my research and study that would diminish this prophetic truth. Everything has confirmed it! There is nothing in Scripture and nothing in who we are as a people that prohibits the U.S. from becoming a backslidden America and the beast/superpower John saw in the last days.

Scripture makes it plain that the Jewish nation that experienced first-hand the presence of God, witnessed His miracles and blessings, became so deceived by this clever enemy called Satan that they totally missed the incarnation, when God became man and visited planted earth. It states that Jesus came unto his own and his own received him not.

Has Satan, masquerading as an angel of light, once again used deception to fool huge numbers, as he did the Jews at the time of the first coming of Jesus, into thinking the beast/superpower he is working through has to be some other religion or power, when in reality, it's the country that has been the center of Christianity and many times called "Christian America" that he has his sights set on as we near the second coming of Jesus? If not why not?

My objective is to help provide the spiritual building materials you need to build your spiritual ark of protection as you prepare for the days ahead, and to help save Christian values in America regardless of what society does.

One of my repeated prayers is that the churches of this land will know another powerful move of God's Spirit that will bring about an era of holiness and divine protection. No one finds pleasure in pointing out where our defenses are weak.

I am also aware that, like all my brothers and sisters, I too am flawed. None of us, looking back over our years, can say we always lived as we should. But God in His incredible kindness and mercy has allowed us the privilege of experiencing Christ and sharing in His ongoing work. Maybe we will even be a part of that privileged generation of stewards on duty when our great master makes His triumphant return!

EPILOGUE

HAVE YOU BUILT YOUR SPIRITUAL ARK OF PROTECTION FOR THESE LAST DAYS?

AMERICA which has a strong Christian foundation and has received much Christian teaching is experiencing an overwhelming increase in the spirit of lawlessness, permissiveness, rebellion and selfishness.

WHY?

America is the center of Christianity in these last days. Seeing that his time is short, the enemy is on the attack, dragging down Christian leaders, destroying

Christian homes, destroying Christian values, and attacking the foundation of our nation.

Whether we realize it or not, we are involved in a spiritual warfare that has caused the moral values in America to deteriorate more in this last generation than in all of the previous years of our country's history. This attack shows no sign of stopping. Statistics show it is getting worse.

Jesus warned that as it was in the days of Noah, so also will it be in these last days. "By faith Noah, when warned about things not yet seen, in holy fear built an ark to save his family" (Hebrews 11:7).

Noah was *Salt & Light* in his time and God showed Noah how to build an ark of protection to save himself and his family. Christians need to build their ARK OF SAFETY for these end-times. Not a physical ark like Noah, but a spiritual ark.

The teachings I wrote in the book *Salt & Light* will help equip you with the spiritual building materials you need to build that ark for you and your family. This book is based on spiritual principles that work for our times. They are spiritual principles that will help you live in spiritual safety despite the enemy's brutal attacks .These principles taught from the Word of God have stood the test of time even during a period when our country's moral values have deteriorated so dramatically.

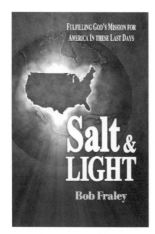

The book
SALT & LIGHT:
*Fulfilling God's Mission for
America in These Last Days*
is a 6 X 9 trade size book
with 281 pages.

CONTENTS INCLUDE:

	Quantity	Total

Salt & Light . . . . **$14.95 ea** . . _____ _____

The Day That Changed America . **$ 6.95 ea** . . _____ _____

Campaign Save Christian America
.40¢ ea. Minimum Order 10 / 25 or more
.30¢ ea. / S&H included. . . . . _____ _____

Prices, Postage	Orders up to $15.00 = $ 2.00	Subtotal _____
& Handling	$ 15.01 - $30.00 = $ 4.00	Postage/Handling _____
Are Subject to	$ 30.01 - $50.00 = $ 6.00	My Donation _____
Change Without	$ 50.01 - $80.00 = $ 8.00	
Notice	Over - $80.00 = 10%	TOTAL _____

Circle payment method:

Check   VISA   MasterCard   AmEx   Discover

_____/_____/_____
Credit Card #   Expiration Date   Signature

_____
NAME

_____
ADDRESS

_____
CITY   STATE   ZIP CODE

_____
YOUR EMAIL ADDRESS
If your shipping address is other than your credit card:

_____
NAME

_____
ADDRESS

_____
CITY   STATE   ZIP CODE

To Order:	**Or, tear out this page**
Call / 1-866-998-4136	**and mail to:**
	Christian Life Outreach
	P.O. Box 31129
Online:	Phoenix, AZ
christianlifeoutreach.org	85046-1129
campaignsaveamerica.com	These books can also
theremarkablerevelation.com	be purchased at your
	bookstore